Praise for *The Social Entrepreneur's Playbook: Pressure Test Your Start-Up Idea—Step One*

"Social entrepreneurship represents an innovative and effective mechanism for addressing many problems around the world. *The Social Entrepreneur's Playbook* is an important contribution to help aspiring entrepreneurs take the first step."
—**David Bornstein, author of *How to Change the World:**
  ***Social Entrepreneurs and the Power of New Ideas* and coauthor**
  of *Social Entrepreneurship: What Everyone Needs to Know*

"*The Social Entrepreneur's Playbook* provides invaluable insights into how best to foster truly sustainable enterprises that are economically viable and that significantly improve quality of life for individuals and communities."
—**Kenneth C. Frazier, chairman of the board, president,**
  and CEO, Merck & Co., Inc.

"The processes recommended in *The Social Entrepreneur's Playbook* show that due diligence matters, and can be carried out, for organizations that attend to those in need. That way, resources can be focused, and well-meaning but vainglorious resource expenditures avoided. What's more: MacMillan and Thompson clearly walk their talk; rather than simply publishing a book, they are pressure-testing their own first draft and asking readers to help write the final manuscript."
—**Mark O. Winkelman, senior director, Goldman Sachs Group, Inc.**

"*The Social Entrepreneur's Playbook* shows us how to understand, evaluate, and pragmatically fund investments designed for significant social impact. It is essential reading for those who care about deploying philanthropic and impact investing resources for the greatest good."
—**Ronald D. Cordes, board member, ImpactAssets, and co-chairman,**
  Genworth Financial, Inc.

"I have long felt that we can do better by using our altruistic resources to build self-sufficiency instead of dependency. *The Social Entrepreneur's Playbook* shows that it can be done and how to do it."
—**Robert B. Goergen, chairman and CEO, Blyth, Inc.**

"MacMillan and Thompson have delivered a powerful set of tools for anyone interested in creating scalable, positive social impact while conserving resources through disciplined entrepreneurship. *The Social Entrepreneur's Playbook* provides a unique and compelling framework for funders, investors, and others who would like to increase the reach, efficacy, and investment transparency of their contributions."
—**Arthur D. Collins Jr., retired chairman and CEO of Medtronic, Inc.,**
  and senior advisor to Oak Hill Capital Partners

The Social Entrepreneur's Playbook

*Pressure Test, Plan,
Launch and Scale Your Enterprise*
Expanded Edition

Ian C. MacMillan
James D. Thompson

Wharton
DIGITAL PRESS
Philadelphia

Published by Wharton Digital Press
The Wharton School
University of Pennsylvania
3620 Locust Walk
2000 Steinberg Hall-Dietrich Hall
Philadelphia, PA 19104
Email: whartondigitalpress@wharton.upenn.edu
Website: wdp.wharton.upenn.edu

Ebook ISBN: 978-1-61363-030-3
Paperback ISBN: 978-1-61363-032-7

Our deepest thanks to the Wharton alumni who have sponsored this program, including the Ambani, Collins, Durrett, Gruber, Holekamp, Hurst, Meyer, Poole, Rosenstein, Snider, and Trone families for their interest, commitment, and willingness to support work in a space so fraught with uncertainty.

This book would not have been possible without the concerted efforts of many social entrepreneurs. In particular, we owe a debt of gratitude to Ilona for her tenacity, candor, and commitment to working with us over such an extended period of time. Alicia Polak made key contributions to the elaborations of frameworks within the manuscript.

Thanks also to Marc Gruber of the College of Management of Technology at École Polytechnique Fédérale de Lausanne for his support in this research.

The Social Entrepreneur's Playbook

Please visit
wdp.wharton.upenn.edu/books/social-entrepreneurs-playbook
to download forms to help you with
your project assessment and planning.

Contents

**Phase Three. From Probable to Plannable:
Launch and Scale Your Social Enterprise**

A Personal Note

On June 18, 2013, Wharton Digital Press published *The Social Entrepreneur's Playbook: Pressure Test Your Start-Up Idea— Step 1*. We provided the ebook for free to more than 10,000 active and aspiring social entrepreneurs as part of what publishing industry blog *ThinReads* called "one of the more unusual ebook ... experiments of the year."

We used our own start-up-to-scale-up method to publish *The Social Entrepreneur's Playbook* because the book is itself a social enterprise: it seeks to generate modest, self-sustaining revenues from book sales while helping social entrepreneurs start up their ventures with less risk and a greater likelihood of success while helping others. The free ebook introduced readers to the first phase of testing a social enterprise start-up idea: defining the social problem and articulating the revenue-generating solution, developing a qualified advisory group, defining and segmenting a seed target population, identifying the most competitive alternative, and addressing the operating realties.

We invited readers of the free ebook to join the Social Entrepreneur's Playbook Advisory Group by taking a survey. This crowdsourced feedback helped shape the complete edition of the book, which you now have in your hands or on your screen: *The Social Entrepreneur's Playbook: Pressure Test, Plan, Launch, and Scale Your Social Enterprise—Expanded Edition.*

Nearly 300 readers joined the Social Entrepreneur's Playbook Advisory Group, many of whom are aspiring and active social entrepreneurs and philanthropists. Their ranks include founders, CEOs, executive directors, managing directors, and other leading social entrepreneurs and supporters. Members hail from for-profits and nonprofits and from all around the world. For a list of the advisory group members, see the Acknowledgments.

In addition to providing feedback on the free book, members of the advisory group shared where they were in the start-up process, what their biggest challenges were, and what they needed to know to be successful. The expanded edition you are now reading covers the issues that the advisory group told us are important. It includes the complete three-phase method for successfully testing, planning, and launching and scaling a social enterprise.

If you have read the free ebook, you will still want to start at the beginning of this book. Phase one has been expanded to include advice on setting revenue and social impact goals, how to navigate the inevitable sociopolitics, how to develop a strong concept statement, and more.

We wrote this book to share what we have learned over the past 12 years while working with social entrepreneurs. We want to broaden the impact beyond those we work with directly by assisting anyone devoting resources to helping the less fortunate, wherever that might be, in making a positive social impact and generating an income while doing so.

Thank you for reading this book. We wish you all the best with your social enterprise.

For updates, downloadable forms, and additional information for nonprofits, please visit wdp.wharton.upenn.edu/books/social-entrepreneurs-playbook.

Introduction
The Creation of Social Wealth Out of Poverty

"If you don't know for sure what will happen,
but you know the odds, that's risk. …
If you don't even know the odds, that's uncertainty."

—Frank Knight[1]

In 2000, Ilona's social enterprise was launched in northwestern Zambia, a region that was suffering widespread unemployment precipitated by a collapse of copper prices followed by the closing of Zambian copper mines, which in turn had led to widespread malnutrition.[2] Her idea was to find ways to reduce the price of animal feeds (heretofore affordable only to larger-scale chicken producers), thereby creating a whole new market (small-scale chicken farmers), enriching the local economy (by creating new jobs), and reducing malnutrition (small-scale chicken farmers would keep some of the chickens for their families while selling the bulk at local markets), all the while building her own business (as small-scale chicken farmers succeeded, they would continue to buy chicken feed from her company).

She began Zambia Feeds in a shed, with six men mixing feed by hand on a concrete floor. The company produced just enough feed per month for her first few customers. Six years later she stood on a mezzanine platform in her new warehouse and threw a switch at a ceremony to inaugurate newly commissioned equipment that would mix, pelletize, and pack nearly 2,000 tons of chicken feed per month, which was destined to be sold to a growing group of self-employed farmers, who would then sell their chickens at local markets. Now her business was serving 1,600 independent farmers, many of whom had sprung from the ranks of the unemployed, and who were now employing one or more workers themselves. The feed Ilona was selling would translate into approximately 40 million daily protein portions per year of chicken meat from chickens reared by these farmers. This number would eventually grow to 70 million daily protein portions per year. Ilona launched an enterprise that helps thousands of people, creating nutrition and employment through self-sufficiency, while at the same time generating tidy but not excessive profits through the phenomenon of social entrepreneurship.

Social entrepreneurship has rapidly become a mainstream topic and field of interest spanning the boundaries of academia, entrepreneurship, nonprofits, and the economic development sector. Organizations worldwide are testing new approaches to attempt to alleviate poverty and other social problems (whether in emerging economies or in often large pockets of poverty embedded in advanced economies). These organizations—be they nonprofits (increasingly under financial strain), for-profits (looking to combine corporate social responsibility with growth possibilities in bottom-of-the-pyramid environments), or public-private partnerships—have begun launching revenue-generating enterprises to carry out their social missions. These "social entrepreneurs," as they are generally called, have captured the interest of business schools (every major business school now offers courses in social entrepreneurship); books and magazines ("doing well and doing good" is one of the hot topics in the business press); philanthropic organizations; and, recently, economic development and foreign aid agencies, which are helping to launch these new hybrid businesses, or are promoting partnerships with them. Yet despite such pervasive interest, little is known about how to make such ventures work, or why some fail and others succeed.

To find out for ourselves, we entered this space in 2001 as a first step in creating what is now the Wharton Social Entrepreneurship Program. We work on the ground in Africa and in the United States with social enterprises—organizations created to address and alleviate a social problem by generating a revenue stream. Our goal has been to study the challenges of building dual- or multiple-objective business models under conditions of high uncertainty. Since venturing into this space, we have seen firsthand the challenges of social enterprises. Some of our enterprises have been quite successful, others not, and still others have developed or spun off in unanticipated directions.

Our experience has led us to conclude that there is both good news and bad news for social entrepreneurs. First the bad news: these organizations face daunting odds as they try to create wealth where currently only poverty exists. Doing business in areas where markets have failed means high levels of uncertainty that often leave well-intentioned social entrepreneurs blindsided by unexpected problems. Not surprisingly, one study of revenue-generating ventures launched by nonprofits finds that very few actually make money.[3] Moreover, the same study discovered "a pattern of unwarranted optimism" when examining how nonprofits evaluate possible ventures.[4]

We did promise good news: Despite the dark picture we've just painted, the odds are not insurmountable. Our years in the field have introduced us to social enterprises, such as Zambia Feeds, that are quietly making a real impact on society and earning modest net revenues. Our work has proved that it is possible to launch a successful social enterprise—by taking small steps, focusing on discovery versus outcomes, and being constantly vigilant for the unexpected. The insights we have gleaned from our field experience are the basis for the ideas we present in this book.

The process we have developed does not guarantee success. It does, however, increase the chances that, inexpensively and early on, you will be able to spot those ventures that simply won't make it and refocus your energy on those that may just have legs, at the same time reducing the cost and consequences of those that fail.

Who Should Read This Book?

This book is for anyone who wants to create and run a social enterprise that generates revenues or, better yet, profits while alleviating social problems. However, despite the revenue-driven perspective we cover, the principles and tools in this book will also benefit any of the following organizations:

- Agencies and charitable organizations attempting to deliver poverty alleviation directly;
- Foundations and nongovernmental organizations (NGOs) facing increasingly distressed pleas for funding from the agencies and charities they support, while themselves facing reductions in resources;
- Established firms seeking to deliver meaningful corporate social responsibility (CSR) programs or, more selfishly, to build future markets at the Bottom of the Pyramid;[5]
- Venture capital firms and impact investors with a social orientation; and
- Donors and philanthropists interested in enhancing the impact of the funds they donate.

Social Entrepreneurs: Addressing Social Problems with Revenue-Generating Solutions

The fundamental purpose of the social enterprise is to address a social problem and generate revenues in so doing. The way the Wharton Social Entrepreneurship Program does this is to generate revenues, preferably net revenues,[6] thereby reducing dependency and increasing the self-sufficiency and sustainability of an enterprise. After 12 years working on the ground with social enterprises, we conclude that they typically function in environments much different from more traditional entrepreneurial enterprises. One major difference is the perceived level of risk. It's not that social entrepreneurs face more risk than traditional entrepreneurs; they face greater uncertainty. Although the two terms are often used interchangeably, the concepts underlying them are different: risk is measurable; uncertainty is unknowable, and therefore immeasurable.

Why this higher level of uncertainty? We point to three main factors:

1. Social entrepreneurs target highly intractable social problems. If the problems were not intractable, some profit-seeking enterprise would already be earning income by resolving them (or exploiting the opportunity).

2. Instead of simply entering a market, the social entrepreneur often needs to create a market where none yet exists.

3. Social entrepreneurs work in uncharted environments that, by their very nature, generate uncertainty. All the enterprises we worked with met some of, if not all, the following challenges:

   - **Undeveloped markets.** Nascent markets typically offer entrepreneurs or firms little idea about what beneficiary/customer segments to target and what the reactions of those segments might be.

   - **Uncertain pricing.** Given that the market is weak, there is scarce indication of what prices might be acceptable for the products or services envisioned by the social entrepreneur. Furthermore, there are few proxies available to provide price baselines or bands of comparison.

   - **Absence of consistently administered (predictable) governance.** Entrepreneurs can confront mazes of ambiguity when they try to navigate the corridors of permissions, people, and policies. Interpretations of legal frameworks and their corresponding requirements can be frustratingly unclear and often ad hoc.

- **Unreliable infrastructure.** Nonexistent, poorly developed, or poorly maintained infrastructure often translates into unacceptably high operational costs and high unreliability of transportation, power, water, and labor.
- **Untested technology.** The use of a technology, especially a new one, in an undeveloped market environment adds additional complexity to the venture, and the new technology is unlikely to work as it did in its original environment and likely will need to be modified to adapt to local conditions. Even then, acceptance is not guaranteed.
- **Unpredictable competitive responses.** In environments with significant market failures, the nature of competitive response may be very different from that in more developed markets. For example, over the last two decades in southern Africa, we have regularly seen the burning or shooting-up of taxis and buses competing for a share of fares between new informal (and unregulated) settlements and the cities to which commuters need to travel. The "combatants" have little concern over whether the vehicles contain passengers.

Our research and fieldwork show that given the uncertainties involved in trying to create a solution via social enterprise, potential solutions must be "funneled" in a way that systematically reduces their intrinsic uncertainty ahead of major resource commitments.

At the start of an initiative in such uncertain environments, there are many conceivable approaches, all of which may be equally *possible*. The first challenge is to configure, from among the many possible approaches, those that are *plausible*, and then to reduce the uncertainty of these plausible approaches to the point where probability distributions can be assigned to outcomes,[7] thereby making the approaches progressively *plannable*—that is, developed to the point where more conventional risk assessment and valuation methods can be used. This process of moving from uncertainty to risk (simplified as Figure I.1) creates a basis from which to experiment and learn. The process is designed to help identify those ideas that may "have legs" (success potential), guiding the social entrepreneur toward a feasible business model (if one exists). It also helps identify, early on, those ventures that will likely fail, allowing the social entrepreneur to abandon the idea at little cost (either financially to the entrepreneur or to the potential beneficiaries) and move on to other potential ideas.

Figure I.1: Moving from Uncertainty to Risk

From Possible to Plannable— A Process for Social Entrepreneurs

Moving from uncertainty to acceptable levels of risk requires a different approach from that normally adopted by traditional entrepreneurs. In particular, it requires significantly more pre-work, experimentation, reality checks, and planning. Much like a sieve works, we propose a process of continual feasibility checks and low-cost trials en route from possible to plannable, ideally having the sieve hold back the less doable ideas and letting the most viable ones pass through to the next level. In essence, the process is that of an enterprising mind-set.

This front-end work of remorselessly redirecting or abandoning ideas is crucial for two reasons. First, resources available to address social problems are limited, and are becoming more so every day, so it is a tragedy if they are vaingloriously wasted. Second, the cost of failing later on in the process may have grave consequences for the potential beneficiaries, who are often left to flounder when a venture or aid program runs out of funding and pulls up stakes. Figure I.2 outlines our process for developing social enterprises.

This book addresses each phase of the process. We have framed the book in a way that will constantly guide you in preserving your scarce resources and help you do more with less—a perspective in keeping with our earlier work[8] and one that shares elements of the

Figure I.2: Building Social Enterprises: A Process

**High levels
of uncertainty**

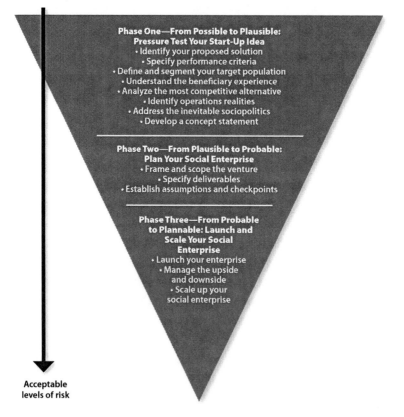

**Phase One—From Possible to Plausible:
Pressure Test Your Start-Up Idea**
- Identify your proposed solution
- Specify performance criteria
- Define and segment your target population
- Understand the beneficiary experience
- Analyze the most competitive alternative
- Identify operations realities
- Address the inevitable sociopolitics
- Develop a concept statement

**Phase Two—From Plausible to Probable:
Plan Your Social Enterprise**
- Frame and scope the venture
- Specify deliverables
- Establish assumptions and checkpoints

**Phase Three—From Probable
to Plannable: Launch and
Scale Your Social
Enterprise**
- Launch your enterprise
- Manage the upside
and downside
- Scale up your
social enterprise

**Acceptable
levels of risk**

newly resurgent "lean thinking" trend in innovation. At this early stage, you are spending your imagination and time, rather than your funds or those of your supporters.

- **Phase One: Pressure Test Your Start-Up Idea.** To enable you to progress from possible to plausible, we will help you analyze a proposed revenue-generating solution to a social problem; specify performance criteria; define and segment your target population or beneficiary; understand the beneficiary experience; analyze the most competitive alternative; identify operations realities; address the inevitable sociopolitics; and, finally, develop a concept statement.
- **Phase Two: Plan Your Social Enterprise.** To support you in your move from plausible to probable, we will explain how to frame and scope the venture, specify deliverables, and establish assumptions and checkpoints.
- **Phase Three: Launch and Scale Your Social Enterprise.** To help you go from probable to plannable, we show how to launch your enterprise, manage the upside and downside, and scale your enterprise.

We end each chapter with two short sections: a Chapter Checklist and a Tough Love Test. The Chapter Checklist tasks you to review what you have done to make sure you are ready to go forward. The Tough Love Test asks a series of challenging questions for which only a positive response will justify your going further with your project.

Social entrepreneurs must beat enormous odds to create a business that alleviates widespread social problems (malnutrition and unemployment) while making meaningful net revenues (when she retired, her enterprise earned a 12% return on sales). For Ilona, moving from 6 employees mixing feed by hand to 200 employees working in a semi-automated facility required immense discipline and a rigorous process to navigate the high degree of uncertainty she faced from the get-go. We strongly believe that social entrepreneurs who follow the principles and processes we outline in this book put themselves in the best possible position to achieve success in this challenging arena.

From Possible to Plausible: Pressure Test Your Start-Up Idea

CHAPTER 1

Articulate Your Targeted Problem and Substantiate Your Proposed Solution

In 2012, when Ilona retired from the poultry feeds business she had started with six men mixing feed with shovels in a shed, the social enterprise she had built was producing more than 3,000 tons of feed per month—enough to support nearly 2,000 small-scale poultry farmers whose combined output delivered nearly 70 million daily protein servings per annum to their communities. To do this, Ilona had to overcome the manifold uncertainties we described in the introduction. What the rest of this book will do is lay out the systematic process we developed from our fieldwork with Ilona and others, a process that will help anyone concerned with using minimal resources to accomplish the greatest good in any organization set up to assist those in need. This process can be (and we believe should be) used by managers of social enterprises, by managers of NGOs and nonprofits, by large firms entering the Bottom of the Pyramid space, and by philanthropists interested in seeing that their philanthropic funds have maximal impact.

Given that social entrepreneurs confront such high levels of uncertainty, we suggest that from the very beginning you adopt a learning approach by initially spending a serious amount of time systematically researching the problem and substantiating the feasibility of your solution; discussing it with people in the know; and bringing to the table a willingness to be open to what your research tells you.

One of the biggest mistakes social entrepreneurs make is to charge in with inadequate understanding both of the problem they want to address and of the practicability of the solution they have in mind.

The first step is crucial: carefully articulate the problem and your proposed solution. This step has three components:

1. **What is the social problem I wish to address?**
   - Who is suffering?
   - What are they suffering from and when?
   - What's causing this suffering?
   - How many people are affected?
   - Where are they located, and how are they geographically distributed?

2. **What is my solution?**
   - How will my enterprise alleviate the problem?
   - Who and how many will benefit?
   - What major costs will be incurred?
   - If it is to be a business, how will revenue (income) be generated? If it is not to be a business, how will operating funds be secured?

3. **What will beneficiaries have to do differently for my proposed solution to work?**
   - This is very important: What behavior changes am I seeking on the part of the target beneficiaries?
   - In particular: How difficult will it be for us to effect these behavior changes?

To illustrate these three components of the first step, let's look at Ilona and Zambia Feeds.

Articulate the Problem/Solution: Zambia Feeds

When Ilona approached what was to become the Wharton Social Entrepreneurship Program about a severe malnutrition and unemployment problem in the Copperbelt and northwestern provinces of Zambia, she explained to us that the region, with approximately 2 million inhabitants, had experienced up to 50% unemployment at times over the previous two decades, mainly because of copper mine closures. Furthermore, those out of work did not have easily transferable or marketable skills. Without money, they couldn't afford food (particularly food rich in protein) for themselves and their families. With her experience in animal husbandry and animal feeds, Ilona chose poultry farming as the start to a solution—small-scale poultry production doesn't require advanced skills and needs very little capital investment.

The largest cost (approximately 70% of the cost of goods sold) of producing poultry is the feed consumed by the fowls. At the time, national poultry production was dominated by a few established commercial growers, who sold their meat in larger, wealthier urban areas. Ilona observed that the existing suppliers of feed mixes were geographically distant and produced what she believed to be lower-quality products, with a resultant lower yield in animal output. Furthermore, she believed the incumbent feeds producers to be oligopolistic, overpriced, and indifferent to the potential of two highly underserved market segments: subsistence farmers and small-scale commercial poultry producers in the rural areas remote from the major towns. If she could find a way to produce and distribute higher-quality feeds for a lower price, she could team up with a company already producing cornmeal and flour and start a feeds business—creating a new market for small poultry producers in remote northwest Zambia, who, as they built their own businesses, would buy ever more of the product. Of course, she would need to educate her potential new customers (the currently unemployed or underemployed) about chicken farming and its benefits to them and their families.

Thus, she would articulate her problem as follows:

What is the social problem I wish to address?

Malnutrition and unemployment in the Copperbelt region of northwestern Zambia.

- Who is suffering? The large undernourished and underemployed population in northwestern Zambia.
- What are they suffering from and when? Poor nutrition (particularly, low protein consumption). The problem is ongoing.
- What's causing this suffering? Low or no incomes due to poor employment opportunities.
- How many people are affected? Between 500,000 and 1 million, depending on the season and geographic expanse included in the early estimates.

What is my solution?

Develop a commercial feed production business (selling poultry feed) that would open up new rural markets comprising subsistence and small-scale poultry farmers, who could then feed their families (addressing malnutrition) and sell surplus birds in the local markets (generating earnings and employment).

What will beneficiaries have to do differently for my proposed solution to work?

The unemployed and the current subsistence farmers (potential customers, or "users" of her feed products) would need to understand and agree on the benefits of rearing chickens and be willing to learn and execute the entire process of rearing and selling chickens.

Articulate the Problem/Solution: Ikotoilet

Let's turn to a case outside the Wharton Social Entrepreneurship Program to offer a second illustration of the articulation process, namely Ecotact, a private, for-profit company that addresses sanitation problems in developing nations. The company received start-up funds from the Acumen Fund,[9] a nonprofit global venture fund that uses entrepreneurial approaches to solve problems of global poverty. One of its products is the Ikotoilet, a freestanding pay-per-use sanitation center that has since been installed in many towns in East Africa. Here is how articulating the problem would look for the Ikotoilet.

Globally, nearly 2.5 billion people lack access to proper sanitation, half of whom must defecate in open sewers due to lack of infrastructure.[10] This "sanitation system" serves as a virulent breeding ground for cholera and dysentery, resulting in staggering social costs: high rates of morbidity and mortality as a result of diarrheal diseases. In Kenya alone, one in five children under the age of 10 dies of diarrheal diseases. Taking a cue from Mahatma Gandhi, who once said that "Sanitation is more important than independence," Ecotact founder David Kuria challenged himself to find a business solution to sanitation problems in Africa, while at the same time to make a small profit that would at the very least be enough to keep the business sustainable. Kuria realized that while the problem could not be quickly solved globally, it could be addressed at least in East Africa, starting in Kenya.

What is the social problem I wish to address?

Poor sanitation in East Africa, beginning with Kenya.
- Who is suffering? The densely concentrated urban populations of the region.
- What are they suffering from and when? Relatively high levels of preventable, debilitating, and often fatal gastrointestinal diseases such as diarrhea. The problem is ongoing.
- What's causing this suffering? Poor sanitation is a persistent culprit for infection.

- How many people are affected? Approximately 9 million (22% of the total population of 43 million).

What is my solution?

Build sanitation stations (Ikotoilets), initially in Kenya, and expand later throughout East Africa, which users could access on a pay-per-use basis.

What will beneficiaries have to do differently for my proposed solution to work?

Kuria's problem was that even if he charged very little, would he be able to compete with a system that, in the eyes of many people, was basically free? Potential users (customers) were currently "paying" nothing for sanitation services—they simply defecated in sewage pits or in the street at night. It was going to require a significant amount of effort both to educate potential toilet users and to convince them that what they thought they were getting for "free" actually came at great social cost (e.g., morbidity and mortality caused by fecal-borne disease). This is a typical "tragedy of the commons" situation: "Even if I do pay to use the toilets, if others do not, infection will continue."

Once you have put together your initial description of the social problem, your solution, and the beneficiaries' required behavioral changes, you can analyze your population of proposed beneficiaries to identify the different segments of the population and target which segments you will engage with first, as your seed segment, and why. This will be covered in the next chapter.

Establish Plausibility Criteria

Establishing a defining set of criteria that your business must meet to justify moving forward is one of the most powerful ways to prune out implausible ideas, saving precious resources for the more plausible ones.

Two types of criteria shape such pruning. We deliberately use the "pruning" metaphor; your yield of fruit is much larger and of much higher quality if you prune a fruit tree back to fewer high-yielding branches instead of letting it grow uncontrolled and wild, which results in a paltry yield.

Screen-Out Criteria: Your Institutional Disqualifiers

Screen-out criteria are what you use to disqualify automatically any proposed project, no matter what other redeeming features it has. These are really tough criteria and should be kept to a minimum. A project that fails even one of these criteria is presumed to be doomed from the start or totally in conflict with your values, and therefore should be dropped. A project that incurs even one such disqualifying condition should automatically be screened out unless you can come up with a strategy to mitigate the offending condition.

The Wharton Social Entrepreneurship Program's list of disqualifiers was developed over the 12 years we have worked with social entrepreneurs in the United States and several African nations. We will screen out any venture:

- That generates dependency rather than self-sufficiency;
- That will be located in countries where corruption (and/or bribery) is rampant, deeply embedded, and not able to be circumvented;
- Where any necessary equipment is not highly robust, simple to operate, and easy to repair;
- Whose operations require a large percentage of employees to have advanced technical qualifications;*
- Where (eventually) the net revenues from activities are insufficient to cover *replacement* of assets;
- Where workers or partners involved in the project will earn less than the nationally stipulated minimum wage;

---

*This is particularly important in rural Africa and other developing regions.

- Where a pilot business cannot be launched and run at low cost;
- Where you do not believe you will successfully effect the requisite beneficiary behavior change; and
- Where U.S. or host country laws will be transgressed.

Note that these disqualifiers need not be *your* disqualifiers. You surely will want to generate your own. But to the extent that you create similar disqualifiers, you certainly will reduce the number of costly and ultimately unsuccessful projects you undertake.

Note also that we have had to turn our backs on many projects, often with enormous regret, but we have thereby also been able to avoid pouring resources into what would have ended up as unsuccessful efforts.

Screen-In Criteria: Conditions That Increase the Attractiveness of a Project

Screen-in criteria are those that we believe enhance the attractiveness of projects. Unlike with the screen-out criteria, where the presence of only one disqualifies the project, the more screen-in criteria present, the more attractive the project becomes. In other words, screen-in criteria are cumulative builders of attractiveness, and if you score competing projects on these project-boosting criteria, you can use their total scores to choose among those projects. We have also found it useful to use the criteria as a creativity trigger, asking what we might be able to do to enhance a project along the criterion being considered.

Our screen-in criteria include the following:
- The number of people who will be helped will be high (instead of dozens, perhaps hundreds, if not thousands, of beneficiaries).
- The direness of the problem to be attacked is high (the reduction in suffering is high).
- The project has large long-term benefits.
- Key stakeholders will be highly supportive of the project.

- Beneficiaries are highly receptive to the solution.
- The degree of on-the-ground experience of the team is high.
- Experience of the lead entrepreneur is extensive.
- Testing on a small scale (low cost, short time frame) is easy.

Note: We emphasize the importance of low-cost testing by including it on both the screen-out (reject any project that cannot be tested at low cost) and screen-in (the easier it is to test, the more attractive it is) criteria.

You can convert these criteria into a scoring table to compare competing projects in terms of attractiveness (if you have a number of potential projects in mind or different approaches to the same project). For example, Table 1.1 shows how the Zambia Feeds project fared on the screen-in criteria.

Table 1.1: Screen-In Criteria for Zambia Feeds

	Very low > Very high
Number of people who will benefit	1 2 3 4 ⑤
Suffering of beneficiary as a result of problem	1 2 ③ 4 5
Long-term social impact potential of project	1 2 3 4 ⑤
Degree of key stakeholder support for project	1 2 ③ 4 5
Receptiveness of beneficiaries to solution	1 ② 3 4 5
Degree of local knowledge and experience of team and/or advisors	1 2 3 4 ⑤
Degree of entrepreneurial experience of management	1 2 3 4 ⑤
Ease of testing on a small scale (low cost, short time frame)	1 2 3 ④ 5
Total Score	**32 of a possible 40**

Scoring allows you to see problems you may need to resolve before moving ahead. In this example, Ilona anticipated a fairly low receptiveness level on the part of the beneficiaries: people might feel inadequate to the task of raising small batches of chickens for sale or for their own consumption. If she felt she couldn't do anything to change this, she would not have launched the project. She decided, however, that through a series of informational seminars in villages and with the support of influential resident community members, she could get the buy-in from enough farmer recruits to start her company. The success of the first farmers would ramp up attendance at subsequent seminars, where she would respond to questions from newly minted farmers.

In high-uncertainty environments, this set of preliminary filtering criteria is a key weapon for driving down the probability and incidence of failure. Our 12 years of experience on the ground have shown us that the presence in a project of any one of the *disqualifying conditions* we use will at best severely cripple if not kill a project. Ideas are limitless; time and resources are not. By identifying and killing disqualified projects from the get-go—and not later, after you have expended energy and wasted resources—you will have the resources to launch projects with higher chances of success. Projects that survive the disqualifying screen can then be rated for their screen-in scores. If you have only one project, you can develop screen-in scores for major locations or customer segments and select the highest-scoring segments to focus your start-up.

Start to Assemble an Advisory Group for Purposes of Validation

Now that you have begun to build a sense of the problem and the possible solution to it, you must consider whether you have advisors with adequate on-the-ground knowledge of the environment. If you do not have people with such knowledge on your project already, you need to identify and recruit them now. The role of this group, at this stage, is primarily to provide concept validation and market insight.

Begin with one or two knowledgeable advisors to act as sounding boards. As your venture progresses, you can augment your advisory group with appropriate and useful members (start small and snowball) and, in so doing, build an influential support group to provide concept validation, implementation guidance, and help on stakeholder management.

In the Zambia Feeds case, Ilona first made certain she had the support of the CEO of the milling company with whom she had teamed up to implement the project and of a salesperson from the region in which she would be launching. As the venture developed, she gradually augmented her informal board of advisors with experts in animal nutrition, veterinary science, and feed production systems. By the time the venture was ready to scale, she had built a formidable advisory group of influential people from both within and outside her region of operations.

Once you have secured the advice and support of your first experienced advisors, you can begin to dig more deeply into the context and environment of your proposed beneficiaries.

Chapter Checklist

Following the processes outlined in this chapter, you will have:
- ○ Articulated the social problem.
- ○ Articulated the proposed solution.
- ○ Articulated what the beneficiaries will need to do differently for your solution to work.
- ○ Developed disqualifying criteria for screening out highly vulnerable ideas and screen-in criteria that will enhance the plausibility and attractiveness of the project.
- ○ Started to assemble an advisory board and begun validating your problem and proposed solution with the board.

Now we ask you to subject your idea to the first of the Tough Love Tests you will encounter in this book. The idea is to challenge yourself to make sure you have done the homework needed to avoid going forward with a poorly formulated venture and thereby wasting scarce resources on a project doomed to failure.

Tough Love Test

If you answer no to any of the following questions, you should seriously reconsider your idea. If you answer no three times or more, you should drop the idea. It simply won't be worth your time and resources if you cannot surmount the challenges at this early stage. If you answer yes to all the following questions, by all means, continue exploring your idea.

1. Are you confident that you have specified the full dimensions of the social problem with respect to its scope, dispersion, and distribution?
2. Are you confident that you have identified a solution that will work in the context of the environment where your product or service is going to be delivered?
3. Have you carefully thought through any changes in behavior your beneficiaries will need to make in order to benefit from your solution? Are you confident that you will eventually be able to effect that behavioral change?
4. Does the proposed venture avoid your screen-out criteria?
5. Does the proposed venture score high on your screen-in criteria?
6. Have you begun to develop an advisory group of people "in the know"?
7. Have you discussed your project's feasibility with your advisory group, which should comprise people who are knowledgeable about the environment and people knowledgeable about the social condition you are tackling?

CHAPTER 2

Specify Performance Criteria

I f your idea still looks plausible, you can now turn to performance expectations, which comprise your specifications of social impact and financial outcome.

Unit of Social Impact

You need to decide on a unit of social impact, which specifies how you will measure the benefits being delivered by your program, such as lives saved, disease cases cured, number of children able to read, food available and consumed, and so on. Specifying the unit of social impact forces you to think about how you are going to rate your performance and measure it, and thereby, how you are going to communicate to the world and stakeholders (people who have a vested interest in your outcome) what social impact your project is delivering. It often requires a lot of (perhaps uncomfortable) thought to come up with a clearly articulated measure by which you and others will be able judge the social value and contribution of your enterprise.

A way to approach this is to revisit your problem analysis and solution and think of an outcome metric that will measure the impact you intended. The challenge is to select a unit of social impact measurement that closely correlates with your desired social benefit. For instance, Ilona of Zambia Feeds reasoned that an adequate way of reflecting an easing of hunger and malnutrition was to estimate the number of daily protein portions per year that would result from the consumption of the chickens of growers who purchased her feed. While not precise, this unit of impact goes straight to the social bottom line: every pound of chicken feed sold yields an estimable poundage of chicken meat that can be consumed by the population in her target area.

Kuria of Ecotact had a more difficult problem: It is virtually impossible to measure the reduction of disease resulting from his Ikotoilets; the social impact of prevention is always difficult to measure. What he could do is measure the number of uses of his facilities. Then, for purposes of estimating actual social impact, he could use available data from sources such as the World Health Organization to infer the number of infections and deaths avoided by the use of his toilet facilities. While such data may not provide precise estimates, they do provide a plausible basis for reasonable estimations of infections and deaths avoided.

Unit of Revenue

For financial performance, you need to decide on the unit of revenue, namely, the elements for which payers will pay and thus generate the revenues needed for operating the project. Examples of revenue units are items sold, paid service hours delivered, and paid contracts completed. As we note later in this chapter, the beneficiary is not necessarily the one who pays. In the case of Ilona's project, the revenue unit she selected was a 25 kilogram (kg) bag of feed purchased by a chicken farmer; in the case of Kuria's Ikotoilet, the revenue unit was a single use of his Ikotoilet.

Before you go any further toward starting the actual project, it will pay off handsomely to discuss your proposed metrics with potential stakeholders, getting their buy-in so that they are assured that you will be disciplined and that they can track your progress.

However, such stakeholders will be interested not only in how you are going to monitor performance, but also in what levels of social impact and financial performance you hope to achieve. And before you can realistically decide on the levels of outcome you intend to achieve, you need to examine realistically:

- What you need to be able to do to deliver your social impact, and
- What the reaction will be by those who will be affected by the success of your project.

Upcoming chapters attend to these issues: Chapter 4 is devoted to deciding what activities and capabilities will be needed to actually deliver your intended social impact, and chapter 5 is focused on analyzing key stakeholders who could materially influence the venture outcome. Once these assessments have been done, we can turn to setting minimum realistic performance targets for the venture.

Beneficiaries Are Not Necessarily the Ones Who Pay

In social-entrepreneurial settings, the beneficiary is not necessarily the person paying for the product or service. In many cases, a third party—maybe a governmental or nongovernmental organization—will pay. If this is the case with your idea, you will need to take into account how likely the third party is to pay and their capabilities to do so. It may be useful to use the language users and payers rather than customers.

In the case of nonprofits, while you may not be generating business-like sales revenues, the cold reality is that there has to be a source of funds to support your operations. For a nonprofit, the funding unit needs to be specified in place of a revenue unit. This funding unit might be an average annual donation, an average annual grant approved, or even the securing of one major grant annually, but you need to specify the key measures you will use to monitor progress in securing sufficient funds, at minimum, to cover the total costs of operations.

An example of this is the Hippo Roller. Traveling around Africa, social entrepreneur Grant Gibbs was struck by the amount of time and effort women villagers spent collecting water. In poor, rural communities a water source may be many miles away, and walking there to collect the day's water needs is backbreaking (almost literally), hugely time-consuming work that is delegated primarily to women. Gibbs wondered about the effects of this work on women. Beyond the physical degradation to their bodies (many women in Africa suffer from premature spinal aging because of this work), this work also prevented them (and their daughters) from going to school or working. Gibbs devised a simple, elegant solution: a barrel-shaped strong plastic container that can hold 90 liters (24 gallons) of water with a handle attached to the axis of the barrel allowing the user to either push or pull the barrel. His beneficiaries (users), however, did not have the money to pay for the barrels. Instead, Gibbs decided to go to sponsors (payers), such as the World Food Programme and other NGOs, who in return for their sponsorship (i.e., paying for the production and distribution of the rollers) would have their logos printed on the round caps that seal the barrels. In this case, therefore, the revenue unit becomes a batch of funded rollers with a sponsor's logo; and the unit of social impact is the roller itself, with the imputed hours of water-carrying saved and a reduction in physiological damage. In his planning, therefore, Gibbs takes into account how many batches of rollers he is required "sell" to third parties (payers) in order to accomplish his social goals in assisting users.

Gibbs has undertaken a redesign of the roller in recent years. Once again, its original use is morphing into other uses, and it is attracting other users: in certain locales, the Hippo Roller is now also being used as a base for mobile retail kiosks, where shelves are mounted on the roller axle and fixed on the handle above the roller, which then serves as the mobile shop's wheel. It is also being used by small-scale produce farmers to roll their produce to market, the roller being cheaper and far more navigable over poor-quality, muddy roads than a bicycle.

In the Wharton Social Entrepreneurship Program, we first determine the appropriate metrics and then decide on what the minimum required performance targets are in order that the venture deliver goals considered worth the time and effort of all those involved.

This approach allows us to develop and model any proposed venture before launching it. In the planning stage, we will show you how to set these minimums and then how to scope, frame, and build a venture operations model prior to investing in the actual venture. We prefer that our modeling show us if our assumptions about the impact of a new venture are wrong, so the venture can fail or be redirected on paper before failing in the field—it is cheaper that way.

Chapter Checklist

Following the processes outlined in this chapter, you will have:

- ○ Decided on units of social impact to measure social impact (by which you intend to measure and monitor social performance progress) and discussed and validated it with potential supporters.
- ○ Decided on a revenue unit (by which you will measure and monitor financial performance progress) and discussed and validated it with potential supporters.

With this in mind, you can now turn to the Tough Love Test.

Tough Love Test

If you answer no to any of the following questions, you should seriously reconsider your idea. If you answer no three times or more, you should drop the idea. It simply won't be worth your time and resources if you cannot surmount the challenges at this early stage. If you answer yes to all the following questions, by all means, continue exploring your idea.

1. Are you confident that the proposed unit of social impact is appropriate for measuring and monitoring progress in achieving social outcomes? Does your advisory board agree?
2. Are you confident that the proposed revenue unit is appropriate for measuring and monitoring progress in achieving financial outcomes? Does your advisory board agree?

3. If the beneficiaries will not be paying for the product or service, have you identified one or more other parties who will pay for it?
4. Do these parties agree with your proposed unit of social impact and revenue units?

CHAPTER 3

Define and Segment Your Target Population

Next you need to define a population segment to start with in order to further test your idea. Again, pursue small starts and learn before investing much money. Ask yourself: Who of the proposed beneficiaries are most likely to adopt my offering? Where are they located? Are enough of them willing to adopt my offering to warrant my efforts and demonstrate evidence that my concept is sound? Is reaching them possible at an acceptable cost?

Segment Your Target Market

Your beneficiary population is unlikely to be completely homogeneous, and targeted segmentation of the population is critical for increasing the chance of early traction. The idea is to think of a subset of your beneficiaries with whom you hope to gain as rapid an acceptance as possible at minimal cost. One way is to select a target segment that scores highly on a "willingness to adopt" measure. The 10 attractiveness features listed here are those we used to develop a score sheet for different segments of the beneficiary population. This list can be used as a starting point for your endeavor, but should be modified, as you learn, to reflect your specific case.

Ten Attractiveness Features Increasing Willingness to Adopt

1. Their perception of the need to benefit: Are they aware of their need for your proposed benefit?

2. Connectedness of actions to positive outcome: Do they clearly recognize the link between the actions you propose and the expected positive outcomes?
3. Salience to customer: How much does the need matter to them?
4. Urgency to customer: How long might they postpone having the need satisfied?
5. Visibility of benefit: How easy is it for them to see the benefit?
6. Timeliness of effect: How quickly is the effect of the benefit observable?
7. Credibility of the benefactor: How much do they believe your solution will help?
8. Performance contingency: How sure is the solution to work?
9. Reversibility of effect: If the benefit stops, does the problem return?
10. Fundability of the benefit by or for them: Can they afford the solution, or will someone else pay for it on their behalf?[11]

These generic attractiveness features work well with most projects, but are neither mandatory nor exhaustive. In creating your own list, you may want to remove features that don't fit your venture or add those that fit your venture more closely.

From your version of this list, generate a score sheet to compare the market segments on their views of the potential solution. To create the score sheet, first identify several types of potential beneficiaries (or customers). In the case of Zambia Feeds, the first three segments Ilona identified were (i) large commercial producers, (ii) small-scale producers, and (iii) villagers (free-range growers).

Define and Segment Your Market: Zambia Feeds

Ilona felt confident that she fully understood the potential beneficiaries of her enterprise, and the competitive landscape she was entering. Having grown up in the area, she was very familiar with local customs, language, and sociopolitical conditions, thus she possessed great insight into which beneficiaries might be most likely to adopt her idea. She also had the advantage of having worked in agriculture and animal husbandry, which gave her key insights into her competition, including their geographic location and concentration, distribution reach, and pricing schemes. Her initial target customer segment, or beneficiary segment, was the small-scale, primarily rural subsistence farmers interested in improving their lives without having to relocate. To further test her intuition, however, she created a table (Table 3.1), based on the list of 10 attractiveness features.

You need to develop a set of criteria (attractiveness features) for your choice of segment, though it may be useful to start with the ones we used or the ones in the following tables, weeding out any that are inappropriate for your project and adding any that are germane to you.

Scoring is done as follows: As you go down the list of attractiveness features, rank how the relevant segment stacks up against each feature. A ranking of 3 is the highest, 2 is medium, 1 is low.

The objective of this exercise is to see which segment is most attractive, and therefore most likely to get traction, so that it can be assessed as a possible seed segment for which you launch your enterprise. Based on this table, it is clear that the most promising market segment, and therefore the seed segment to start with, is the small-scale chicken producer, which scored 22. Once the company was established, Ilona would be positioned to encourage the next-most-promising segment—namely, villagers rearing free-range chickens—to buy her feed and then build small-scale chicken coops after they were convinced of the merits of the proposition. Selling to larger commercial producers would have to wait, if she attended to them at all.

Table 3.1: Segment Attractiveness Factors—Zambia Feeds

	Large commercial producer	Small-scale producer	Free-range villager
1. Pervasiveness—scale and scope of the segment need	1	2	3
2. Acceptance of your offering by customer and other key players	1	3	2
3. Salience to customer— Is the need your solution meets important to the customer compared with other needs?	1	2	3
4. Urgency to customer— Is it important that the need be satisfied soon, or can it wait?	1	2	1
5. Visibility of benefit— Can the satisfaction of the need be easily observed?	2	3	1
6. Timeliness of effect— Can the need be quickly satisfied by your offering, or will it be delayed?	1	2	1
7. Credibility of your company— Is it seen as legitimate, qualified, and competent?	2	1	1
8. Performance contingency— Is your solution sure to work?	2	3	2
9. Competitiveness of your solution—How does it fare against alternative solutions?	1	2	1
10. Fundability of the purchase and use by segment—Is your solution fundable?	3	2	1
Total	**15**	**22**	**16**

Define and Segment Your Market: Ikotoilet

For the Ikotoilet solution to be accepted, beneficiaries would need to change the way they thought about sanitation. Potential users/customers were currently paying nothing for sanitation services; they simply defecated in open sewage areas or in the street at night. It would require a significant amount of work both to educate potential buyers and to convince them that what they thought they were getting for free[12] was actually costing a great deal in the long run (e.g., in morbidity and mortality caused by fecal-borne disease).

Potential Market Segments

Although the problem is widespread throughout the world, Kuria, founder of Ecotact, chose to begin in Kenya, a country he knew well, and within a specific city, namely Nairobi. Now he had to find a market segment that could see the value of his solution and that had the means to pay for it. There appeared to be three potential beneficiary types, based on population location:

1. **Local markets.** Generally outdoor markets where people buy and sell goods and services. Public toilet pits can be found in many of these markets, but they are generally extremely unhygienic. People coming and going to markets generally have some, though perhaps not a lot of, money.

2. **Central business districts.** Administrative and commercial centers of towns where one finds government offices and small to large businesses. Some buildings have their own toilets, but others do not. People visiting the town and people who work in buildings without toilets are generally obliged to use municipal toilets, many of which are free but generally badly maintained, highly unsanitary, and in some cases very unsafe. The people in these districts generally have some money.

3. **Estates/townships.** Large "ghettos" that have very little in terms of infrastructure. Residents are overwhelmingly poor,

and personal safety is a major concern, especially at night. Some have communal toilet pits, and others have no sanitation whatsoever. Many residents resort to "flying toilets": plastic bags defecated in and then hurled into the street after dark.

Table 3.2 rates each of these potential markets in relation to selected aspects of Kuria's proposed solution.

Based on the criteria, central business districts and local markets emerge as the segments where the Ikotoilet could get early traction. Over time, the project could eventually be migrated to the estates/ townships. The scores for the central business district and the markets are close, and much higher than that for the estates/townships. Kuria chose central business districts as the seed segment to demonstrate feasibility. But the major impact would be on markets, and eventually the estates/townships. As the project took hold, he focused on markets and then found that bus stations were major areas where toilet facilities could be offered at low prices to people who had some money and a need for privacy.

In your case, you will need to decide which of the 10 (and any other project-specific) attractiveness features fit your particular project and then generate a table similar to Table 3.2. Here it would pay to get input from your advisory group and people knowledgeable about the problem, and/or the location in which you intend to attack the problem, to help you identify key segments, formulate criteria, and rate the segments on those criteria.

Again, do not spend huge amounts of time building these scoring tables and arguing over close scores. When operating in conditions of high uncertainty, you would rather be "roughly right" than "precisely wrong," particularly in the early days, as you learn your way into the new venture. Ecotact's Ikotoilet is a fascinating example of how, as the uncertain project unfolded, the locations in which it was executed (bus stations) were different from those expected.

Table 3.2: Segment Attractiveness Factors—Ikotoilet

	Local markets	Central business districts	Estates/ townships
1. Pervasiveness—scale and scope of the segment need	3	2	3
2. Acceptance of your offering by customer and other key players	2	3	1
3. Salience to customer— Is the need your solution meets important to the customer compared with other needs?	2	3	1
4. Urgency to customer— Is it important that the need be satisfied soon, or can it wait?	3	1	1
5. Visibility of benefit— Can the satisfaction of the need be easily observed?	2	3	1
6. Timeliness of effect— Can the need be quickly satisfied by your offering, or will it be delayed?	2	1	3
7. Credibility of your company— Is it seen as legitimate, qualified, and competent?	2	3	1
8. Performance contingency— Is your solution sure to work?	2	3	1
9. Competitiveness of your solution—How does it fare against alternative solutions?	2	3	1
10. Fundability of the purchase and use by segment—Is your solution fundable?	2	3	1
Total	**22**	**25**	**14**

Chapter Checklist

Following the processes outlined in this chapter, you will have:
- ○ Specified some major beneficiary segments.
- ○ Generated a set of attractiveness features against which your segments were scored (starting with our list, but tailoring it to your project).
- ○ Applied the attractiveness features to those segments.
- ○ Articulated a high-scoring seed segment with which you could test-launch your idea.
- ○ Discussed the market and segments with your advisory group.

With this in mind, now turn to the Tough Love Test.

Tough Love Test

If you answer no to any of the following questions, you should seriously reconsider your idea. If you answer no three times or more, you should drop the idea. It simply won't be worth your time and resources if you cannot surmount the challenges at this early stage. If you answer yes to all of the following questions, by all means, continue exploring your idea.

1. Are you and your advisors satisfied that you have developed meaningful project-specific attractiveness features for scoring the attractiveness of your beneficiary segments?
2. Are you and your advisors confident that you have identified distinct segments of your beneficiary population that will respond differently to your proposed solution?
3. Have you scored these segments according to your attractiveness features, as in Tables 3.1 and 3.2, and selected a target segment with which you estimate you will get the most traction early in the launch?
4. Have your advisory board members agreed that this specifically articulated population segment is the target segment with which to test your idea?

CHAPTER 4

Understand the Beneficiary Experience

I t's easy to get excited about an idea—one that you think is going to change the world. Yet seemingly great ideas are often received with indifference, if not outright rejection, by their intended beneficiaries. Why this frequent disconnect?

Many would-be social entrepreneurs grow up and first work in developed nations and later attempt to create solutions for emerging nations or for pockets within their own nations characterized by grinding social woe. This outsider status frequently results in a misunderstanding of the market and of the "need" for one's solution.[13]

If you view the challenges of others through your own lens of limited contextual understanding, you run the risk of proposing a solution that is not deployable in the beneficiaries' environment. In a case involving attempts to stem HIV/AIDS in Africa, cultural naïveté (at best) or cultural arrogance (at worst) illustrates this lack of contextual insight. In the early 1990s it became clear to many Western NGOs and governments that the condoms they were distributing in African nations were simply not being used. The conventional wisdom in the West was that the populations in these nations were in denial, or simply being fatalistic by choosing not to use condoms.

Susan Watkins, a professor of sociology at the University of Pennsylvania, thought there had to be more to the story. She followed the same group of women in Malawi from 1991 to 2005 to better understand their views of HIV/AIDS and condom use, documenting conversations they had with one another, whether at the local water source or in small groups in the fields or the village. She found a very active population of women who were keenly aware of the ravages of AIDS. Only, the Western panacea of "give them condoms" ignored deeply ingrained social norms, and the fact that many women wanted to have children (women's fertility is highly valued in most African nations) and many were afraid their husbands, if forced to use condoms, would leave or evict them.

Cultural naïveté or even arrogance often leads to one of the most common and critical business mistakes: having a product orientation rather than a beneficiary orientation. A product orientation means that you charge ahead creating the offering you want without taking into account what the users want, expecting them to readily accept what you have to offer. Safeguarding against this requires a keen understanding of the potential beneficiaries of your solution and how *they* see the "problem" you have identified. In the rest of the book, we emphasize the idea that your challenge is to "sell" your offering into a population of (perhaps unconvinced) beneficiaries. We shall often speak of the beneficiary of your effort as a "customer" in a "market" for your offering in which there is "competition" in the form of alternative options for the beneficiary.

To repeat: One of the biggest mistakes an entrepreneur can make is to have a product rather than a beneficiary (or customer) orientation. To avoid having a product rather than a beneficiary orientation, the first step is to take a serious look at the offering from the perspective of the beneficiaries by systematically thinking through the *entire* set of experiences your target segment must go through in order to derive a benefit from your offering. It is amazing how many projects fail because well-intentioned individuals or groups neglect to look at those projects from the point of view of the people they aspire to help.

Beneficiary Experience: Zambia Feeds

Ilona, like any other entrepreneur, could not simply assume that producing and selling high-quality, low-cost feed would result in the production of chicken meat. She would need to recruit and train locals to use her product (animal feed) to raise their chickens.

These farmers would need to go through many steps before the feed they purchased could be converted into chicken sales at the local market. Before farmers can sell chickens at market, they must transport those chickens to market, and before that, rear the chickens, which means they must:

- House them;
- Feed them;
- Water them;
- Keep them warm;
- Vaccinate them; and
- Keep the facilities clean (biosecurity).

And before rearing them, they must:

- Purchase chicks (from a third-party supplier) to be fed.

And before that:

- Store feed.

And before that:

- Transport feed to a poultry house.

And before that:

- Purchase feed.

And before that:

- Raise funds to start rearing.

And before that:

- Learn how to rear chickens.

And before that:

- Decide to rear chickens.

And before that:

- Hear about the poultry rearing program.

Get the idea? Beneficiaries may need to do an awful lot to experience the benefit of your solution, especially if, up to now, the only alternative to your offering has been for them to do nothing but endure their situation. Systematically thinking through what the beneficiary needs to be able to do to experience the benefit of your solution can be mapped into a Beneficiary Experience table (see Table 4.1).

Table 4.1: Beneficiary Experience Table for Zambian Poultry Farmers

Hear about poultry-rearing program.

Decide to rear chickens.

Learn how to rear chickens.

Raise funds to start rearing.

Purchase feed.

Transport feed to poultry house.

Store feed.

Purchase chicks (third-party chick supplier needed).

Transport chicks to poultry house (possible third-party transportation needed).

Rear chickens:
- Keep housing clean (biosecurity).
- Vaccinate them (third-party veterinarian needed).
- Keep them warm.
- Water them.
- Feed them.

Slaughter some fowls for home consumption.

Consume chicken.

Transport surplus chickens to market.

Sell chickens at market.

Manage income.

Beneficiary Experience: Ikotoilet

For comparative purposes, let's look at the simpler Beneficiary Experience table for Ecotact's Ikotoilet, depicted in Table 4.2.

Table 4.2: Beneficiary Experience Table for Ikotoilet Users

Hear about Ikotoilet.
Decide to use facility.
Become aware of need.
Get to the facility.
Be instructed in use of facility.
Pay for use.
Use the facility.
Habitually reuse facility.

In Kuria's case, this is a much simpler Beneficiary Experience table. The beneficiaries need to do little other than know about the facility, be convinced to use it, and then regularly use it. With this much simpler Beneficiary Experience table, of course, things were easier for Kuria than for Ilona, but even a simple table such as his can harbor problems. One would think that using a toilet would be quite simple. However, the early Ikotoilet design was challenged as inadequate for use by practicing Muslims, for its lack of a shower attachment or other device for post-use cleansing.

With the Beneficiary Experience table fleshed out, it is time to talk to your advisory group and have them challenge your Beneficiary Experience table. You should also seriously consider talking to a number of target beneficiaries to get their reaction to your idea of what the experience of your project needs to be for them to accept it—a step that the ill-fated condom programs should probably have undertaken.

Chapter Checklist

Following the processes outlined in this chapter, you will have:
- ○ Defined the requisite beneficiary experience and associated activities.
- ○ Generated a Beneficiary Experience table, and had it accepted by your advisors and discussed with beneficiaries.

Tough Love Test

If you answer no to any of the following questions, you might want to rethink your idea. If you answer no twice, abandon your idea—it simply won't be worth your time and resources if you cannot surmount these challenges at this early stage. If you answer yes to all the following questions, by all means, continue exploring your idea.

1. Do your advisors agree that you deeply understand what the proposed beneficiaries are doing *currently* to manage/endure their problem?
2. Have the advisors signed off on your proposed Beneficiary Experience table?

CHAPTER 5

Analyze the Most Competitive Alternative

Having tried to understand what a beneficiary will need to experience, now ask yourself: What is the most competitive alternative already out there? That is, who currently offers the best alternative approach to the problem? Put differently, how do beneficiaries currently cope in the absence of your envisioned product or service? This chapter focuses on helping you think through the direct and indirect competition for your proposed solution and pinpoint whether your venture is sufficiently different from, and superior to, what is currently available. Are you attempting to deliver a substantively superior experience or something only incrementally different from an available alternative?

In the case of Zambia Feeds, some farmers mixed their own feeds from locally sourced raw materials, which made them Ilona's indirect competitors, even though they were also potential customers. The more extreme case was free-range chicken producers, who sporadically scattered corn grit but generally expected their chickens to forage for themselves, and who provided only a primitive protective enclosure for their chickens to take shelter and sleep, and who did not require a supply of "imported" chicks, leaving chick production to Mother Nature.

Another possible source of competition for an enterprise might be government or NGO programs that subsidize a product or service you intend to provide. In such cases, you may find it extremely difficult to compete with or "match" what in effect are indirect competitive solutions to your idea. You may even have direct competitors already providing a somewhat different offering. Such competition provides valuable benchmarking information such as price, product or service features, and distribution channels. It also offers a platform for questioning during research as you try to determine what about your envisioned offering would need to be different and/or superior in order for beneficiaries to support it. Do not lightly dismiss competition as not being present. As we have mentioned before, it may be that the beneficiaries' current alternative is simply to endure their problem. This alternative, though it may be frustrating for you, is nonetheless competitive, and is frequently present for nutrition-, education-, and health-related deprivations. In fact, in some cases, beneficiaries' fatalistically *doing nothing at all* itself constitutes an entrenched competitive alternative that you may have to overcome.

As you look at the most competitive alternative, if your solution appears to come up short against it, ask yourself if and how you can *innovate* to provide a significantly superior offering. If you cannot, scrap the project—don't squander scarce resources replicating what is already being done! Innovation can come in many forms, from innovation in delivery to innovation in payment systems. One of the most famous innovations in business dates back to 1856, when the Singer sewing machine company in New York introduced the "hire-purchase" plan, the prototype for all future installment loan plans, thereby forever enabling people of limited means to make purchases for which they do not have cash.[14] The idea opened up an entire new market of low- and middle-income consumers, who would use money earned by sewing and selling garments to pay off their sewing machines, rather than paying up front in cash they did not have.

Nearly 150 years later, the largest cement manufacturer in Mexico, CEMEX, took similar steps, with similar success. During Mexico's economic downturn in the mid-1990s, CEMEX saw a major drop in domestic sales. The formal segment (contractors and builders) dropped roughly 50%, while sales in the informal segment (do-ityourselfers) dropped just 10% to 20%.[15] Realizing it was missing out on a huge market—the informal market for cement has a potential for $400–$500 million annually[16]—CEMEX turned the existing cement-buying process on its head. The company experimented with a new program called Patrimonio Hoy (or "Your Heritage Today"), giving the poor access to the materials they needed to build their houses. With this innovative project initiated in 1999, CEMEX opened a multitude of small kiosks throughout Mexico to be closer to its customers, using the opportunity to explain credit and building practices to them. It then helped local neighborhoods raise funds and provided them with a small team, including an architect, to facilitate construction. In return, the communities purchased cement from CEMEX to build their houses. The program was both philanthropic and profitable. By 2005, more than 100,000 houses had been built by and for low-income Mexican families, and CEMEX had received greater than $42 million in total sales.[17] CEMEX now has similar programs generating homes self-built by the poor in more than a dozen developing countries.

Both Singer and CEMEX innovated by having a beneficiary-centric, instead of a product-centric, orientation. It is vital that you carefully consider what you propose doing from the perspective of the user, or beneficiary, you have in mind, and that you ask yourself, "Is what I am proposing *truly* a superior and attractive alternative to the current situation?" If your answer is yes, then the sooner you are able to get concept validation from the intended beneficiaries, the better. If no, then either stop what you are doing or consider how you might transform the current situation into one with more compelling incentives for the intended beneficiaries. Should you wish to read examples of transformative moves made by firms across geographies and industries, we suggest you refer to the book *MarketBusters*,[18] by Rita McGrath and Ian MacMillan.

Most Competitive Alternative: Zambia Feeds

As we showed in the Zambia Feeds case, Ilona's seed customer segment comprised existing small-scale producers. The most competitive alternative for these small producers was for them to buy and mix their own (lower-quality) feed, using seasonally available raw materials, and to forgo the benefits of higher production yields (much-better-quality meat) and thus higher selling prices and therefore higher cash flows. We also showed that for the *longer term*, the highest potential lay in persuading village farmers to put together a small chicken coop (or to use a spare room under cover or an unused hut) and rear chickens as a profitable enterprise using the more productive Zambia Feeds product.

In the right-hand columns of Table 5.1 on pages 39-40, we have listed the advantages of farming using Zambia Feeds versus two existing competitive alternatives: the "seed segment" (existing small-scale producers), some of whom are mixing their own feed; and the "longer-term" segment (villagers with "free-range" chickens). For the free-range villager segment, reality kicks in: It is clear that any farmers Ilona recruits are going to have to invest considerable effort and incur some expenses compared to simply having a flock of chickens running free and foraging around their village. For existing small producers mixing their own feed, the challenge is to convince them that Zambia Feeds will in fact deliver attractively higher cash flows stemming from faster and greater yields of better-quality meat.

Most Competitive Alternative: Ikotoilet

Next let's look at Ecotact's Ikotoilet, as shown in Table 5.2 on page 41, remembering that the seed target beneficiaries are members of the public frequenting the central business district without access to clean toilets. The longer-term major target segments are the local trading markets for goods and services, and eventually the residential estates/townships.

Table 5.1: Beneficiary Experience Table for Small-Scale Zambian Poultry Farmers

Beneficiary experience	Advantages of Zambia Feeds program	Advantages of existing small producers (who already farm, mixing own feed)	Advantages of villagers with small flock of free-ranging fowls foraging for themselves
Hear about program.			
Decide to rear poultry.			
Learn how to rear poultry.	Much better meat quality		
Raise funds to start.			No funding costs
Purchase feed.	Much higher quality premixed feed	*Disadvantage: has to source ingredients and mix own feed*	No funding costs
Transport feed to poultry house.		Lower transport costs (some raw materials)	No transport costs
Store feed.		Lower spoilage costs	No spoilage costs
Purchase chicks.			No chick costs
Transport chicks to poultry house.			No transport costs
Rear chickens.	Much higher yield		
Keep housing clean (biosecurity).			No cleaning costs
Vaccinate them.	Lower disease losses	Lower disease losses	No vaccination costs
Keep them warm.		No fuel costs	No fuel costs
Water them.		No water feeder costs	No water feeder costs
Feed them.		Lower feed costs	No feed costs

Table 5.1 continued on next page

Table 5.1: Beneficiary Experience Table for Small-Scale Zambian Poultry Farmers *(Continued)*

Beneficiary Experience	Advantages of Zambia Feeds program	Advantages of existing small producers (who already farm, mixing own feed)	Advantages of village with small flock of free-ranging fowls foraging for themselves
Slaughter some fowls for home consumption.			Cheaper to rear and consume
Consume chicken.	More higher-quality meat faster		
Transport surplus chickens to market.			No transportation of chickens
Sell chickens at market.	Much higher prices and greater income	Some income	*Disadvantage: no income from chickens*
Manage income.		*Disadvantage: less income*	*Disadvantage: less income*

Note: For purposes of greater clarity, we occasionally insert a disadvantage of a competitive alternative versus the proposed offering by flagging it as a disadvantage and by entering this disadvantage in italics.

Is Your Offering Competitive?

If what you propose to offer is not meaningfully superior, different, or attractive (after validation by your advisors), you need to reconsider your offering prior to attempting to launch. If we consider the Zambia Feeds Beneficiary Experience table, it is clear that two of the critical differences between the existing small producer alternative and Zambia Feeds' proposed activities are the ability of the small-scale farmer to generate larger quantities of higher-quality meat more quickly, and to extract a price premium and greater cash flows once the grown chickens have been sold at market. In order to enable this, Zambia Feeds needed to be sure it had the capabilities required to sell high-quality feed at a low enough price such that farmers

Table 5.2: Beneficiary Experience Table for Ikotoilet Users

Beneficiary experience	Advantages of Ecotact's Ikotoilet	Central business district: Advantages of established municipal toilet	Markets: Advantages of open pit (or holding it in till finding a ditch or bush)
Hear about. Ikotoilet.			
Decide to use facility.			
Become aware of need.			Disadvantage: prolonged discomfort
Get to facility.			Disadvantage: hard to find a suitable spot
Be instructed in use of facility.			
Pay for use.		No need to pay	No need to pay
Use the facility.	Avoid infection and disease	Disadvantage: unsanitary and often does not work; dangerous	Disadvantage: no privacy; highly unsanitary
Habitually reuse facility.	Avoid infection and disease	Disadvantage: exposure to disease	Disadvantage: huge exposure to disease

could make a profit. The visible success of the program for the small-scale producers could then be leveraged to convert some (hopefully many) free-range villagers into small-scale commercial producers. In the case of the village farmer-to-be converts, the advantage is the ability to generate meat for the family and cash for other expenses, but this must be offset by the extremely low cost of free-ranging, which involves zero investment.

A second feature of the tables is that they highlight the behavior changes your target beneficiary would need to make in order to accept your product or service. Consider the HIV/AIDS-prevention program we referred to in the previous chapter. It turns out that the program administrators, in many cases, focused on the proper use and handling of the condoms they were making available, but few tried to affect the highly entrenched behaviors and beliefs that made condoms an extremely unpopular choice among men. Not surprisingly, many of these programs have been colossal failures.

It is worth repeating that there is *always* a competitive alternative, even if the alternative is merely to do nothing.

Now that you have further developed your insights into the beneficiary, you must consider whether you and your advisory group have sufficient expertise to evaluate your current position and assist in your next steps. We highly recommend that you use this opportunity to consult with your advisors in order to determine whether:

- They believe your solution is sufficiently superior to the most competitive alternative;
- They believe it possible for beneficiaries to secure or develop the necessary capabilities required to participate in your program; and
- They can direct you to other suitable advisors whom you might recruit to assist you with additional facets of your enterprise development.

Members of your advisory group should play an active role in the development of your enterprise. The earlier you solicit their help, including in expanding the group itself, the better.

As important as their support is their identification of key risks within the environment early on and help in mitigating and/or overcoming those risks so as to prevent unnecessary barriers and time-consuming delays.

A cautionary note here: It is in your best interest to listen to the advisors you have assembled, but this does not mean you have to blindly obey them. It is not uncommon for the first response to a new and innovative idea to be skepticism. However, there is nothing to stop you from pushing back if you feel you have a powerful counterargument; but you should pay attention to their concerns and be open to suggestions that will alleviate those concerns. This should be done in the spirit of constructive deliberation. Encourage anyone with serious doubts about an aspect of your enterprise to offer a constructive alternative, not just an objection.

Chapter Checklist

Following the processes outlined in this chapter, you will have:
- ○ Developed a Beneficiary Experience table showing the advantages and (in italics) the disadvantages of your enterprise versus the most competitive alternative for your target segments.
- ○ Thought about how you will handle the disadvantages and exploit the advantages for your key segments.
- ○ Confirmed with your advisors that the target beneficiaries can be coaxed into embracing your proposed solution and change their behavior to accommodate the solution you are proposing.

Tough Love Test

If you answer no to either of the following questions, you might want to rethink your idea. If you answer yes to both questions, by all means, continue exploring your idea.
1. Are you and your advisory group confident that you have a plausible and attractive proposition to outperform the most competitive alternative in the key segments you have targeted? (Outperforming means doing *meaningfully better than the most competitive alternative in the eyes of the beneficiary*. If you can't do better than replicate the beneficiary's most competitive alternative experience, your duplication will simply waste valuable resources.)

2. Can you overcome the disadvantages you have in comparison
    with the most competitive alternatives for your target seg-
    ments? Can you clearly articulate how you will do this? If not,
    you should forget about those segments.

CHAPTER 6

Identify Operations Realities

Knowing what the competition has to offer now sets you up for the tough job of thinking through what you will have to be able to *do*, not just say, in order for your program to work. In this chapter, we look at what your enterprise needs to be able to do to make sure the beneficiary experience is actually delivered. What skills, systems, assets, and other resources will you need to deploy to make the whole thing work?

We meet with many well-intentioned social entrepreneurs who have great ideas but who have not thought through all they will be required to do to make their ventures work. It is here that you first begin to boil your concept down to the practicalities of daily operations.

As a first step, you should develop a Deliverables table to outline all the capabilities you will need to have in place so that the benefit can be delivered. Think through the important steps you will need to take for your venture to deliver the required activities. Start off with the steps you outlined in your Beneficiary Experience table in chapter 4 and then lay out all the major steps your project must execute for the whole system to work. Avoid getting lost in too much detail in the early stages; you will revisit and revise your tables and steps more than once as the project unfolds. If you have more than 10 major steps, unless you have a really complicated project, you may be getting lost in unnecessary detail.

Let's return to the Zambia Feeds case. It would have been no good for Ilona just to assume that systems were in place to make happen what needed to happen, where and when she needed it to happen, to make her feeds business operate smoothly. She had to think through every step of the process:

- Raw materials will not magically appear on the doorstep; they will have to be purchased, transported, and stored for use when needed.
- Those raw materials then need to be mixed; the mixing plant needs to be purchased, maintained, and repaired; and spare parts need to be available.
- Materials and equipment can be stolen unless secured.
- The bagged feed mix will not move miraculously from her plant to farmers' doorsteps; it will have to be transported to a place where the farmers can buy it.
- The farmers need to be sure the feed is there when they need it, or their chickens will die.

Note: You simply cannot afford to do a cursory job. There are too many things that can and, more often than not, will go wrong.

So think through what Ilona must do to make sure the beneficiaries can actually experience the items in her Beneficiary Experience table. Before Ilona can have feed available for farmers to buy, she has to follow these steps:

- Buy bags and raw materials, then
- Transport the bags and raw materials to the mixing plant, then
- Store the bags and raw materials, then
- Mix the feed, then
- Bag the mix, then
- Store the mixed feed, then
- Transport the feed to distribution centers accessible to farmers.

Once you have thought through all the steps needed to deliver the business, put them into a Deliverables table. Table 6.1, for Zambia Feeds, lists all the major activities needed for Ilona to be

Table 6.1: Deliverables Table for Zambia Feeds

Recruit and hire labor.

Buy bags and raw materials.

Store bags and raw materials.

Mix the feed.

Bag the mix.

Store the mixed feed.

Transport the feed to the distribution center.

Transport bags and raw materials to mixing plant.

Store the feed at distribution center.

able to deliver the benefits she had in mind. (This is why we call them "deliverables.")

In the case of Zambia Feeds, other, less obvious issues were lurking: If a would-be farmer wanted to start raising chickens, where would she get the chicks? Simply assuming that day-old chicks would be there when needed was not an option. Knowing that they would need to be vaccinated to prevent potentially devastating disease outbreaks was critical. Ilona realized that it was up to *her* to arrange for a supply of chicks and vaccines to be available when farmers came to buy feed. Hence, three more steps in her Deliverables table:

Arrange supplier of chicks for distributors.

Arrange chick delivery to distributors.

Arrange vaccines/vaccination services.

Note: Your tables will evolve as you learn what is required in the field. For the sake of simplicity, this is not included in the tables just given. You will need to be vigilant about updating your tables and the associated financial plans you develop (chapter 9).

For comparative purposes, let's look at the Ikotoilet case (Table 6.2) and see what the entrepreneur needed to have in place for each of his Ikotoilets to work.

Table 6.2: Deliverables Table for Ikotoilet

Secure site property and permits.

Excavate and build facility.

Ensure water and electricity supply.

Build and operate Ikotoilet facility.

Instruct users.

Receive and secure payments from users.

Arrange property guards.

Manage waste recovery conversion to fertilizer.

Sell waste recovery by-products as fertilizer.

This is a good time, once again, to consult with people in the know. Armed with the Beneficiary Experience and Deliverables tables, which have the power of being very easy to explain, seek the input of your advisory group. And remember to challenge them not just to raise concerns and objections, but also to give advice on how to circumvent the problems they raise.

Identify Your Necessary Capabilities

The activities outlined in the Deliverables table will require that you either possess or have ready access to specific capabilities. Identifying those capabilities is important for two reasons. First, you need to be confident that you have or can get the skills needed. Second, capabilities are a key contributor to costs you are likely to incur.

In the spirit of learning ahead of major investment, we capture this information by mapping key capabilities into rows in the Deliverables table. This is an important step. The careful articulation of the skills needed for operations reveals another hard reality of distressed environments: staffing can be a major problem, particularly recruitment, training, and retention of staff conversant in local conditions.

Lack of attention to the capability requirements has doomed many a well-meaning enterprise. In fact, we were speaking recently with a consultant to a social entrepreneur in India who told us that "you have to think about the last ten miles, then the last mile, then even the last ten yards of a delivery."[19] Why? Because myriad problems might occur, including local power failures and lack of emergency power. One social entrepreneurship project in India almost collapsed because the perishable vaccine that the entrepreneur was distributing could not be kept safely and reliably refrigerated due to the unreliability of kerosene supplies for the refrigerators used to store it.

In another example, this one from Africa, a well-meaning nonprofit undertook a reforestation project for which funding was raised, managers hired, nursery space procured, and tree seedlings grown. By the time the nonprofit was ready to plant the seedlings in the area designated for reforestation, however, the rainy season had begun. The rain and mud made it impossible to access and work the reforestation area for three months. Thousands of seedlings continued to grow in the rain—in makeshift locations frantically and very expensively secured after the completely disrupted planting schedule. (Locals, who had not been consulted, were hugely amused that the reforesters were ignorant of the seasonal storms.)

The following Deliverables tables for Zambia Feeds (Table 6.3) and Ikotoilet (Table 6.4) were created earlier in the chapter, but now include a new column listing the capabilities needed to achieve the deliverables. If you do not possess your required capabilities, or know of any way of reliably procuring them (through consultants, outsourcing, or hiring staff), then you may want to think hard about pursuing your venture.

Table 6.3: Deliverables Table with Required Capabilities for Zambia Feeds

Zambia Feeds deliverables	Capabilities needed
Arrange for supplier of chicks.	Identification of and negotiation with supplier
Arrange chick delivery to distributors.	Identification of and negotiation with supplier
Arrange vaccines/vaccination services.	Identification of and negotiation with veterinarians
Recruit farmers.	Marketing and selection skills
Train recruited farmers.	Training skills and chicken-rearing knowledge
Buy bags and raw materials.	Purchasing skills
Transport the bags and raw materials to plant.	Logistics
Store bags and raw materials.	Inventory management
Mix feed.	Superior formulation capabilities Equipment repair skills
Bag mix.	Inventory management
Store mixed feed.	Inventory management
Transport bags of feed to distribution center.	Logistics
Store feed at distribution center.	Inventory management

Ecotact founder Kuria needed very different, more political, regulatory and construction capabilities to build his multi-location sanitation program, as shown in Table 6.4. The point is that unless you really think through the skills that need to be done well to launch and execute the entire Deliverables table, you will find yourself short of skills at a critical, often fatal, juncture as your program unfolds.

Table 6.4: Deliverables Table with Required Capabilities for Ikotoilet

Ecotact deliverables	Capabilities needed
Secure property and permits.	Municipal dealings/relations
Excavate and build facility.	Construction engineering
Ensure water supply.	Civil and chemical engineering Construction engineering
Build and operate Ikotoilet facility.	Construction engineering Sewage treatment
Instruct users.	Instruction
Receive payments.	Cash management
Manage waste recovery.	Waste treatment and recovery
Sell waste recovery by-products as fertilizer.	Industrial selling

Identify Beneficiaries' Necessary Capabilities

You also need to consider the capabilities and skills your *beneficiaries* must have in place in order to make your program work. To do this, go back to the Beneficiary Experience table from chapter 4 and identify the capabilities your beneficiaries need and whether they have them.

Let's return to the Zambia Feeds example and consider the activities a farmer-to-be in the village needs to execute well if her chicken farming is to succeed. See Table 6.5 on the following page.

Now that you have considered the capabilities required by your beneficiaries, revisit the alternatives they have. Think deeply, and candidly, about how superior your proposal truly is relative to the beneficiaries' most competitive alternative. Then consider the effort and capabilities required for the adoption of your offer relative to that alternative.

Think also about how your beneficiaries are going to acquire the needed skills. In many cases, the development of these skills may

Table 6.5: Beneficiary Experience Table with Required Capabilities for Zambian Poultry Farmers

Beneficiary experience	Capabilities/skills for small producers
Hear about program.	
Decide to rear poultry.	
Learn how to rear poultry.	Educational seminars
Raise funds to start.	Loan procurement
Purchase feed.	
Transport feed to poultry house.	Transportation
Store feed.	Storage
Purchase chicks.	Ordering and payment
Transport chicks to poultry house.	Transportation
Rear chickens: • Keep housing clean (biosecurity). • Vaccinate them. • Keep them warm. • Water them. • Feed them.	Hygiene/cleaning Drug dispensing, disease management Temperature management Clean water delivery Feed delivery
Slaughter some fowls for home consumption.	Hygiene, poultry processing
Consume chicken.	
Transport surplus chickens to market.	Transportation
Sell chickens at market.	Sales, cash management
Manage income.	

well end up as your responsibility, which could add considerably to your cost. However, without those skills, the beneficiaries will not benefit—and in turn, neither will you.

Identify Your Costs

In your Deliverables table, you listed all the steps necessary for you to be able to deliver a unit of social impact to your beneficiaries, as well as the capabilities needed to take those steps. Most of those capabilities, however, will most likely incur costs. So your next task is to begin carefully thinking about the resources you will need to accomplish each step in your table.

In Table 6.6, on the following page, we have expanded the number of columns of the original Deliverables table for Zambia Feeds to reflect the kinds of materials, staff, and equipment the venture will need to create and operate the feed plant. Note that, at this stage, we are not estimating the *values* for the actual costs; we are simply making sure we have identified, flagged, and listed the *types* of resources needed, so as not to neglect costs that will be important later.

Determine Your Funding Sources

Once your other tables are completed, we are going to hit you with yet one more! Our apologies, but this table is crucial: it identifies the sources of the funds needed to support operation of your program. In the Zambia Feeds case, Ilona decided that most of the funds would be generated through sales of 25 kg bags of chicken feed. But she also decided that funding for her equipment would come from investment from the Zambia Feeds parent company and funding for inventories from bank loans.

This leads to a simple Funding table (Table 6.7 on page 55). Note that, again, we are not yet quantifying the *amounts* needed, just identifying the *types* of funding sources to be pursued. The task is to review the Deliverables tables to identify all the places where funding will be required, and in the Funding table, to specify how you think the items should be funded.

Table 6.6: Deliverables Table with Types of Costs for Zambia Feeds

Cost types	Equipment	Staff	Materials
From Beneficiary Experience table: Arrange for supplier of chicks.		Manager of feeds company	
From Beneficiary Experience table: Arrange chick delivery to distributors.		Manager of feeds company	
From Beneficiary Experience table: Arrange vaccines/ vaccination services.		Manager of feeds company	
Recruit farmers.		Representatives of feeds company	
Train recruited farmers.		Trainers	Printed materials
Buy bags and raw materials.		Manager of feeds company	Raw materials
Transport bags and raw materials to plant.	Trucks	Drivers	
Store bags and raw materials.	Warehouse, inventory management system	Guards	
Mix and bag feed.	Mixing plant, bagging plant	Mixers, baggers	Power for machinery
Store mixed feed.	Warehouse, inventory management system	Guards	
Transport bags of feed to distribution center.	Truck	Drivers	Fuel
Store feed at distribution center.		Managers/money handlers, guards	Feed inventory

Table 6.7: Funding Table for Zambia Feeds

Funding need areas	Source of funding
Operations	Revenues from feed sales
Equipment	Parent company investment
Inventory	Local banks

In nonprofits the sources of revenues can be more complex, such as grants from governments or foundations, donations from the public, or a combination of these. An example of such a Funding table is Table 6.8.

Table 6.8: Funding Table for a Nonprofit

Funding need areas	Source of funding
Operations	Charitable donations
Equipment	Foundation grants
Land and buildings	Local banks

Chapter Checklist

Following the processes outlined in this chapter, you will have:
- ○ Revisited your Beneficiary Experience table and identified all the activities your enterprise must deliver to ensure that your beneficiaries actually experience what you propose and that what you propose is superior to the most competitive alternative. This is captured in your Deliverables table.
- ○ Identified all the capabilities your enterprise will need in order to execute your solution.
- ○ Started planning how you are going to develop or secure needed capabilities.
- ○ Revisited your Beneficiary Experience table and, in a separate column, identified all the capabilities your beneficiaries need in order to experience the benefits you envisage, and which capabilities they do not have.

○ Started planning how you are going to develop or secure the capabilities your beneficiaries lack.

○ Identified the types of costs you will incur to deliver yours and your beneficiaries' capabilities.

○ Determined your funding sources and noted them in the Funding table.

Tough Love Test

If you answer no to any of the following questions, you might want to rethink your idea. If you answer no more than twice, abandon your idea—it simply won't be worth your time and resources if you cannot surmount these challenges at this early stage. If you answer yes to all the following questions, by all means, continue exploring your idea.

1. Have you clearly identified all the activities your enterprise needs to be able to realize the items listed in your Beneficiary Experience table?

2. Are you confident you can secure access to the capabilities you will need? This would include resources that might normally be readily available in developed countries/situations, such as power, transportation, skills, equipment repair and maintenance, and accounting and recordkeeping.

3. Have you identified the gaps between the skills and resources the beneficiaries have and those they need in order to experience the benefits you propose to deliver?

4. Are you confident that there are ways to close those gaps?

5. Have you identified your potential costs? Are you certain you have or can secure the resources to meet those costs?

6. Have you determined your funding sources? Are those sources reliable and secure?

CHAPTER 7

Address the Inevitable Sociopolitics

I n 2002, Jaytee,[20] a technology entrepreneur, approached us about developing and introducing a new electronic medical decision-making methodology to significantly enhance medical services in countries facing severe HIV/AIDS patient care challenges. Jaytee, who was well connected to the medical, veterinary, and business school community in the United States, had researched several potential African nations and used his list of project-specific attractiveness features to decide where to launch his enterprise, and eventually settled on a country.

The government in that country was actively concerned with improving the health of its citizens. Over the prior 20 years, the country had been ravaged by HIV/AIDS, which had severely debilitated the economy's working population of 18- to 50-year-olds and put a massive strain on the health care system. Jaytee's idea was first to computerize all medical records (then in paper form) and eventually to build an expert system that would enable suitably trained nurses to do HIV/AIDS diagnostic and prescription work, which was then handled by the country's limited pool of highly overloaded doctors. The system, which we shall call AidsAid, would include such activities as diagnosis, first-line therapy prescription decision support, laboratory report follow-up, and patient record management. Jaytee planned to sell the software system to hospitals through government contracts, eventually throughout Africa and later globally. He saw many positives in the idea: by putting many tasks in the hands of nurses, the AidsAid system would significantly increase the efficiency of day-to-day patient care, thus freeing up doctors to focus on the sickest, neediest patients, and ideally resulting in lowered costs for the hospital and better care for patients. To anyone looking from the outside, it seemed like a win-win-win.

Therefore, Jaytee was shaken at the manifold negative responses to his proposed idea. Reactions from people in the health department, in local hospitals, and in public clinics ranged from complete indifference to outright hostility. Then he learned that two years before, a well-established local subsidiary of a multinational software and consulting firm had sold a full-service health care management system to the country's health department. The system had then been force-launched in a number of public hospitals and clinics, at great expense, and was simply not working as hoped. The post-installation challenges caused major disruptions in health care delivery, thereby creating a highly dissatisfied set of stakeholders, who were disillusioned and disgruntled. Fortunately, this system had not been imposed on the private clinics in the country, including the largest one, located in the capital city. The management and staff of this large private clinic were therefore not frustrated by implementation failures. However, they were deeply and understandably circumspect about the plausibility of any electronic system, given the woes they had observed in their public clinic counterparts. Jaytee also experienced resistance from the country's major medical analysis laboratory, which was responsible for the analysis and transmission of all medical tests done for HIV/AIDS patients. Its transmission system was a manual (paper and CD) one, and conversion to an electronic system would have required significant effort on the lab's part, something its management was not yet ready to undertake, since it was comfortable with a manual system that was working well.

The Challenge of Analyzing the Sociopolitical Landscape

In the introduction, we talked about the high uncertainty that social entrepreneurs typically face: imperfect markets, uncertain prices, lack of consistently administered (predictable) governance, unreliable infrastructure, untested technology, and unpredictable competitive responses. In particular, the absence of consistently administered, predictable governance often makes for an extremely punishing environment in which to work. You might, for example, complete all the appropriate application forms to receive a permit to start a business or enlarge a building, only to be told no by the local authorities, with no explanation as to why.

These kinds of bureaucratic headaches happen in every country. However, the minimally resourced social enterprise is more vulnerable to such obstacles, particularly if the start-up disrupts the status quo, and must then defend itself against resistance by entrenched interests. Every one of our projects has been hampered by one or more instances of official inertia, lack of support, bureaucratic foot-dragging, or even outright corruption. In one case, an entrepreneur we were working with attempted to meet a senior government member on six occasions over as many months, only to have every confirmed meeting postponed at the last minute. Whether this was due to corruption or simply incompetence, we never found out, but the delays seriously compromised and almost destroyed the initiative. In Jaytee's case, he was initially almost derailed by unexpected negative feedback from key stakeholders.

A Three-Step Approach to Addressing Sociopolitics

Poor political savvy has destroyed many a well-intentioned enterprise. Analyzing sociopolitics is challenging. You need to use *a lot* of judgment when developing a sociopolitical strategy, but doing so is mission-critical. We recommend the following approach:

1. Identify stakeholders.
2. Categorize your stakeholders: allies, opponents, and needed indifferents.
3. Develop a sociopolitical strategy.

Each project's challenges, and of course yours, will be unique. For instance, you might very much want to block an opponent but simply do not have the wherewithal to do so. Or you might want to mobilize a potential supporter but are not able to generate interest on their part. Unfair as this may seem, our response to such difficulties is to say, somewhat callously, "Life's unfair. Either find another way or stop fruitlessly wasting time and resources."

Identify Stakeholders

To begin the process, start by thinking through all the people and organizations that will be impacted by the success of your venture. Think about parties that will benefit. Think about parties that will experience negative impacts or be inconvenienced. Think about all the parties whose support will be needed. Then think about each party's possible reaction, so you can prepare for the inevitable sociopolitics.

Think of how stakeholders may be affected both negatively and positively. In the real world, there are often cases where stakeholders are conflicted, perceiving both benefits and annoyances from what you are doing.

You will want to capture your thoughts in a Stakeholder Impact table, which will allow you to list the stakeholder, anticipated negative impacts, and anticipated positive impacts. For each impact, note if it is short, medium, and/or long term.

To show how this might look for Jaytee's AidsAid project, see Table 7.1.

Table 7.1: Stakeholder Impact Table for AidsAid

Stakeholder	Major negative impact (if any)	Major positive impact (if any)
Health department	**Short term:** Large potential write-off of existing program; egg on face	**Long term:** Major increase in patient treatment efficacy
Hospital administrator of major private clinic	**Short term:** Installation difficulties with new electronic (in place of paper) system	**Medium term:** Major reduction in workload and increase in medical services
Multinational medical software firm	**Short term:** Potential loss of business and reputation	**Long term:** Possible licensing opportunity with new technology
Doctors	**Short, medium, long term:** Perceived erosion of influence and value of expertise; perceived loss of income (private sector)	**Long term:** More patients handled much more efficiently
Nurses	**Short, medium, long term:** Additional responsibilities	**Medium, long term:** Hugely increased efficacy
HIV/AIDS patient	**Short term:** Perceived risk of "lower expertise" when being treated by a nurse versus a doctor	**Medium and long term:** Increased vitality; potentially longer lifespan, with more time to work and make money
Medical analysis laboratory	**Short term:** Inability to handle lab reporting using electronic records	**Medium and long term:** Much more efficient and accurate record management and transfer

Notice in Table 7.1 that many of the AidsAid stakeholders may be affected both negatively and positively and that the negative effects happen in the short term and that the positive benefits may emerge only after a delay. This is not atypical. Handling this combination of short-term negatives before longer-term positive effects is difficult, but it is further reason to make your table comprehensive.

When you create your own sociopolitical strategy, be aware that your Stakeholder Impact table will evolve over time and will need to be regularly updated as you learn and as stakeholders in the environment begin to hear about, and respond to, your plans.

A good time to revisit your Stakeholder Impact table is when you hit a key checkpoint in your Discovery-Driven Plan, which will be discussed in chapter 11. It is also worth noting that in the mind of stakeholders, particularly those who feel threatened, there is little difference between perceived and real impact. Until such time as an incorrect perception is remedied, you must expect the stakeholders to react and respond to *their* perception of reality.

If completed comprehensively, your Stakeholder Impact table will be a valuable tool for your advisory group members when you discuss your planned activities with them. Bear in mind that your advisory group can be an outstanding sounding board for getting ideas and insights about the reactions of stakeholders as you undertake this rather challenging, perhaps intimidating exercise. If you have chosen them well, the people in the know on your advisory group are the best sources of sociopolitical insight for your specific context. It is critical to engage them early to help you think through the execution of your enterprise.

Categorize Your Stakeholders

The next step in the process is to review your Stakeholder Impact table and begin to categorize your stakeholders. Through our experiences in the field, we identified three important categories of stakeholders that could affect the success of your program:

- Potential allies
- Primary opponents
- Needed indifferents

Potential Allies

Potential allies are those who will benefit from and may be willing to commit support to your project. These people might be transactional partners (such as suppliers and distributors); leaders in commerce; members of local or national government; NGOs and not-for-profits; well-wishers; employees of regulatory or commerce bodies; or local dignitaries, such as tribal chiefs, local healers, or village elders. Among potential allies, you need to identify those who have *meaningful* influence in the market/environment of your project, and think about how to mobilize them, since often they will be the ones you'll most need to help you cope with opposition.

Primary Opponents

Primary opponents are those who will be adversely affected or greatly inconvenienced by your project's success and who also have the wherewithal to resist or delay its execution. Primary opponents who have meaningful power and influence must be identified as early as possible so you can prepare to deal with their concerns and reactions.

Needed Indifferents

These are people or parties who are indifferent to your project's success but whose support, effort, or resources may be necessary, such as government officials responsible for the issuance of permissions, licenses, and certificates. An official responsible for the issue of a license, which legally permits you to operate your enterprise, may have little knowledge of or interest in your beneficiaries or the purpose of your project. Another example of needed indifferents are suppliers and/or distributors who do not see support of your program as particularly beneficial to them financially. Their supplies may be critical to your operations, but the supplier or distributor may see you as "small potatoes," not worth the bother of timely support when supplies are short.

As you begin to categorize your stakeholders, beware of overkill: It is easy to spend an inordinate amount of time generating long lists of stakeholders whose actions are unlikely to have a major impact on your success. Confine your list to no more than eight of the most important stakeholders. If you can't handle the top eight, your project is doomed anyway.

As you saw in Table 7.1, there is a time dynamic at work. In the beginning, few of the stakeholders will be active—after all, you probably have not started your project yet. Still, we have found it helpful to distinguish between players who very rapidly will become active and those who may join the fray later. For simplicity, we distinguish between those stakeholders who are: (i) active or soon to be active when your embryonic program is just starting and is highly (perhaps most) vulnerable; and (ii) inactive and whose active involvement with your enterprise or other stakeholders may be delayed.

At the start, when you are undecided about the category in which to put a specific stakeholder, the fail-safe approach is as follows:

- When uncertain about whether to expect initial opposition, indifference, or support from a specific stakeholder, strategize as if you will experience some initial opposition. In that way, you are not disappointed by lack of support or blindsided by unanticipated opposition.
- When uncertain about whether to expect a rapid or delayed response from primary opponents, strategize as if you expect a rapid response, so you are not caught napping.
- When uncertain about whether to expect early or delayed support from potential allies or indifferents, strategize as if you expect delays, so you are not surprised by a delay or lack of support.

By using these fail-safe approaches, you minimize the damage you suffer if you are wrong.

Returning to the AidsAid example, the following Stakeholder Mapping table shows the allies, opponents, and needed indifferents categorized by whether they are active or inactive. Jaytee needed to think about how much power and influence each particular stakeholder had to advance or retard his program; clearly, he needed to be more concerned with groups that had clout than those that did not.

As with the Stakeholder Impact table, the Stakeholder Mapping table should be updated frequently as your project takes hold.

Table 7.2: Stakeholder Mapping Table for AidsAid

Status	Allies	Opponents	Indifferents
	Active allies to be deployed	*Primary opponents to disrupt or accommodate*	*Needed indifferents to convert*
Currently active (or soon to be be active)		Health department officials who imposed failed electronic system	Medical analysis laboratory
	Potential allies to mobilize	*Potential opponents to disrupt or accommodate*	*Indifferents to convert*
Currently inactive	1. Private clinic CEO 2. Private clinic doctors, nurses	1. Some health department officials 2. Public clinics and their administrators disrupted by weak performance of earlier system	1. Public clinics and their administrators not disrupted by earlier system failure 2. Doctor community 3. Nurse community 4. HIV/AIDS patients

Stakeholders will shift positions, and new stakeholders may enter and exit over time. In the beginning, many groups will fall in the inactive category, but once a business venture begins, some or all stakeholders will become active fairly quickly. (Remember, hornets don't swarm until something disrupts their nest.)

Using Table 7.2, Jaytee is in a position to begin developing a sociopolitical strategy. Let's consider how to go about building such a strategy using a set of specific tactics.

Develop a Sociopolitical Strategy

The next step is to develop a strategy for mobilizing allies, managing opponents, and converting those who are indifferent. You will need to determine if you have the capabilities to influence these groups, whether by mobilizing allies, energizing indifferents, and especially end-running or blocking opponents. If the answer is that you have no way of coping with the reactions of these stakeholders, particularly opponents, it's a pretty good sign that your enterprise will not be viable—at least not in your desired location at this time. Indeed, we learned to our regret in two Wharton Social Entrepreneurship Program projects that failing to plan for these stakeholders leads to significant waste of time, resources, and effort.

To develop an effective sociopolitical strategy, begin by methodically thinking through possible tactics for each major stakeholder, following one or more of the six tactical approaches listed here:

- Specify the response you need from a given stakeholder.
- Identify major current issues occupying that stakeholder's attention.
- Deploy yours or an ally's strategic knowledge, skills, or capabilities germane to the stakeholder.
- Deploy yours or an ally's physical and financial resources germane to the stakeholder.
- Deploy your network connections or expanded network connections.
- In the case of opponents, find a "safe haven" where you can establish a protected position without provoking immediate hostile opposition.

Specify the response you need.

The response you need is what you hope to accomplish with a given stakeholder. It can range from an opponent agreeing to leave you be, through an indifferent agreeing to support you, through an ally committing support or giving you access to their networks in order to cope with other stakeholders.

Identify major current issues occupying stakeholder's attention.

One key to a sociopolitical strategy is to obtain deep insight into what issues are of greatest concern to the target stakeholder. Such issues are not always obvious, and may be unrelated to what you are trying to achieve, but it is *vital* that you understand the broader context of the environment in which you hope to operate. Remember, it is easier for a busy stakeholder simply to say no than to find time and/ or a reason to say yes. Set aside thinking about what matters to *you* and identify the major issues salient to each of your stakeholders, what matters most to them and what is the full context shaping their actions and attitudes. It helps to determine which of your actions they will be most sensitive and reactive to. This will help you better understand the basis of stakeholder opposition, stakeholder support, or stakeholder indifference.

By the way, do not fall into the trap of thinking that because you understand them, and they you, that you necessarily agree with one another. Many people foolishly think, "If only they understood me, they would agree with me." Not true—someone can fully understand you and *still* disagree with you.

You may well find that stakeholders are more concerned with other issues more pressing to them than those addressed by your project. This could have a possible double benefit for you. First, potential opponents may be distracted from attending to your actions while they wrestle with the issues more salient to them. Second, by helping potential allies or needed indifferents with their key issues, you may be able to influence their attitude and behavior with respect to your project.

Deploy strategic knowledge, skills, or capabilities germane to the stakeholder.

See if you have, or can gather, strategic information, or deploy your knowledge or capabilities, to influence the stakeholder. Once you have identified what you consider to be the stakeholder's major issues, use your access to knowledge to do the following:

- **For allies:** Provide them with knowledge or skills or capabilities that will help them resolve their issues, thus earning influence to extract the ally's support where needed, including access to *the ally's allies.*

- **For opponents:** Use your access to knowledge or problem-solving skills to help the opponent on an issue, thus generating influence with them.
- **For indifferents:** Use your access to knowledge, capabilities, or problem-solving skills to improve the indifferent's position on issues pressing to them, in exchange for support you need from them on your enterprise.

You might be able to "horse-trade" with opponents; in other words, provide help or access to solutions to their pressing issues in exchange for concessions on their opposition to your business. Or, more manipulatively (and rarely), you may be able to use your capabilities to aggravate an opponent's position or obstruct the resolution of their issue if they do not provide you with support.

Deploy physical and financial resources germane to the stakeholder.

Think about any physical and financial resources you control (such as property, equipment, funds, and materials) to see if any can be deployed to reward allies and needed indifferents for their support, or opponents for cessation of opposition.

Deploy network connections.

Can you perhaps widen your perspective, looking at your network of contacts and explore opportunities?

- **For allies who cannot help you:** Get access to their allies, who may be able to help you with opponents and indifferents.
- **For opponents:** Use your allies or your allies' allies to neutralize opponents by exposing them, discrediting their argument, marginalizing them, or further compromising their position. Failing this, find a place where the ally can heat-shield you from the opponent.
- **For indifferents:** Get allies to motivate the indifferents' support.

Create a "safe haven."

In the face of very powerful opponents, unless there is some way of using more powerful allies to control them, you may have to accommodate them, and not be allowed to build your program as quickly and/or as widely as you wish. This is the pragmatism of politics. Instead of trying to accomplish your final purpose broadly and quickly, you may have to console yourself with identifying and establishing yourself in a safe haven, a protected niche position where you can get your venture going without being subjected to immediate hostile opposition. This might be a geographic location, such as a part of the country where the opponent has less sway; or among a subpopulation of beneficiaries whom the opponent cannot access; or with particular organizations over which the opposition has no influence—in fact, any subset of the total domain. The idea is to use the safe haven as the starting point from which you will be able to grow over time. This requires that you recognize that you may have to postpone your full impact on the population of target beneficiaries. From your safe haven, isolated from interference, you can build "within-haven" beneficiary support that you can use later on expansion into other regions.

Bring It All Together to Create Tactics

The next step is to create a Tactics table for each stakeholder. Drawing on your Stakeholder Mapping table, start with your most powerful opponents, those who have the clout to block you or slow you down considerably via overt or passive resistance. If you cannot handle these opponents, your project is probably doomed anyway. Your Tactics table for each stakeholder should address one or more of the six tactical approaches we have just discussed:
- Specify the response you want from the stakeholder.
- Identify major current issues occupying the stakeholder's attention.

- Deploy your knowledge and skills to solve the stakeholder's problem or use your knowledge and skills to secure the desired response.
- Deploy your physical and financial resources to reward or aggravate the stakeholder's position.
- Deploy your network or expanded network connections to neutralize opponents, get access to an ally's allies, or mobilize indifferents.
- With opponents, if all else fails, can you find a safe haven away from direct opponent retaliation?

To illustrate this, Table 7.3 shows the process Jaytee went through with the key opponent to his AidsAid project, the government health department.

As a result of this analysis, Jaytee recognized that he was unable to constrain the most powerful, largest opponents and for a period of time would be unable to fully co-opt the health department. However, he recognized that due to access, interest, the absence of an electronic medical record (EMR) system, and the huge benefits for helping them handle patient overload, the largest private clinic in the country could be his first target to sign up. It would serve as a safe haven from health department opponents. As a result of his analysis, he recognized an opportunity to create an ally that would provide him with a safe place from which to build a position. Success with this highly influential ally would then perhaps put him in a position to go back to the government health department with demonstrated efficacy and efficiency for his EMR system. Due to this finding, he then created a Tactics table (Table 7.4) for attending to this potential safe-haven ally.

Through this Tactics table for his major potential ally, Jaytee discovered that the private clinic's deep concern was with uncontrollable patient overload and exploding costs, which would enable him to approach the clinic with a deep understanding of its problem

Table 7.3: AidsAid Tactics Table for Health Department Opponents

Type of support needed: Approval and installation of AidsAid in clinics nationwide

Major current issues occupying stakeholder attention: Current expensive and as yet unsuccessful electronic system

Tactical option	Health department officials
Can you deploy your capabilities to solve opponent's problem in order to build influence for horse-trading? *Or* Can you threaten to deploy your capabilities to aggravate opponent's position?	No No
Can you reward opponent for cessation of opposition? *Or* Can you deploy your resources to threaten to aggravate opponent's position?	No No
Can you use allies or your ally's allies to neutralize opponent or heat-shield your project from the opponent?	No
Can you create a safe haven away from opponent retaliation?	The private clinic cannot be prohibited from installing an EMR system. Perhaps Jaytee can start there and demonstrate viability and efficacy.

and confidence that he could arrange an advisory program that would improve patient management and reduce operating costs.

After addressing his biggest opponent and biggest ally, he was ready to move on to look at tactics for the other stakeholders.

A necessary condition for the system he envisioned would be that all medical records be processed electronically, in order to ensure that the record system he was installing had highly reliable and rapid data utilization. He was aware that the major medical analysis laboratory was still on manual recordkeeping and transmission, and he ran into a resistance problem with the lab's owner. To "convert" this needed indifferent into a cooperative supplier providing electronic rather

Table 7.4: AidsAid Tactics Table for Private Clinic Ally

Type of support needed: Approval, development, and installation of AidsAid in clinic

Major current issues occupying stakeholder attention: Clinic system overload and budget stress

Tactical option	Private clinic CEO
Can you deploy your knowledge and skills?	Jaytee has access to deep experience and skills in operations and financial management, which can be deployed to assist the private clinic in its practice-management challenges.
Can you deploy your physical and financial resources?	No
Can you deploy your network or	Jaytee could arrange via connections with the sister business school of the Ivy medical school to send a team of experienced interns to study, revamp, and update clinic operations.

than paper analytical reports, he worked his way through a Tactics table for this needed indifferent (Table 7.5).

Discussions with the owner of the medical analysis lab revealed that he was concerned with the considerable time and effort it would require to convert his lab from a paper-based system to an electronic one. However, he was also aware that eventually this would have to be done. Jaytee realized that he might be able to send IT trainers from an Ivy medical school program in the country. He was able to persuade the head of this medical school to "lend" a group of people working in the program to train a staff member of the lab in all the skills necessary to operate an electronically based recordkeeping system.

Now over to you. For your primary opponents, potential allies, and needed indifferents, scan your own Tactics table and look for ways to block, avoid, or reduce the opposition of the primary opponent, secure the support of potential allies, and persuade needed indifferents. Try to keep it simple. Complicated strategies are hard to implement, and it is easy to build an overly elaborate sociopolitical

Table 7.5: AidsAid Tactics Table for Indifferent Laboratory

Type of support needed: Electronic uploading, input, transmission, and recording of data

Major current issues occupying stakeholder attention: Lab has inadequate and insufficient IT capabilities and can see future need for this upgrade

Tactical option	Laboratory
Can you deploy your capabilities to solve indifferent's problems in order to secure indifferent's support?	Offer to train lab owner's technicians in electronic data entry, analysis, and recordkeeping. Arrange for IT students at the major university to convert paper records to electronic ones.
Can you deploy your physical and financial resources to entice the indifferent's support?	AidsAid has no such resources.
Can you use your allies or ally's allies in your network to mobilize indifferents?	Jaytee could "borrow" skilled trainers from an Ivy medical school to train lab technicians.

house of cards that collapses under the slightest pressure. The profitable execution of your project will be difficult enough without your resorting to Machiavellian convolutions.

The trick is to identify the top three primary opponents, and use your Tactics table to identify moves to manage, either on your own or with allies, that opposition. Identify your most important potential allies and use the Tactics table to see how to secure their support, either with direct help for your program, or with handling opponents, or with persuading needed indifferents. Then identify needed indifferents, if any, and carry out the tactics development analysis.

In our fieldwork, we discovered a particular type of ally who may be crucial to your success: the godparent. An example might include an influential member of government who is willing to be a heat-shield for the social venture and guide it through the political and bureaucratic landscape. The larger a project, the more valuable it is to have this ally, who can serve as a heat shield with local and national governments. You need individuals and organizations willing to protect your growing enterprise from unnecessary delays and to help you get through the bureaucratic morass when it holds you back, seemingly indefinitely. Failing to identify and secure the support of a godparent is tantamount to condemning your project to death.

Chapter Checklist

Following the processes outlined in this chapter, you will have:

- ○ Determined who benefits from your business and who is at risk of negative impact.
- ○ Identified all stakeholders, even those not directly affected by your business but capable of impacting it, and determined how active each one is or soon will be, and how much clout each has to affect others.
- ○ Identified your key allies and determined whether you have the ability to deploy them.
- ○ Identified your primary opponents and determined whether you have the capabilities to neutralize them.
- ○ Identified needed indifferents and determined whether you will be able to mobilize them.

Tough Love Test

If you answer no to any of the following questions, you might want to rethink your idea. If you answer no more than three times, you should proceed, if at all, with extreme trepidation. It simply won't be worth your time and resources if you cannot surmount the challenges at this early stage. If you answer yes to all the following questions, by all means, continue on to phase two of your idea.

1. Have you and your advisory group identified your key stakeholders (allies, opponents, and indifferents) and do you all agree on what major issues they face?

2. Are you confident you can deploy your allies?
3. Are you confident you can neutralize your opponents?
4. Are you confident you can mobilize the support of needed indifferents?
5. If your project will be large in scale, do you have a "godparent" who can shield you from local and national political intervention?

CHAPTER 8

Develop a Concept Statement

Congratulations! You've taken the bold step of working your idea through the first phase of the social enterprise development process. If you go no further in this book, you have already come a long way. Spending primarily your imagination, you've imposed a rigorous set of Tough Love Tests on your idea and now have a good sense of whether it is at risk of failure (if that's the case, you've lost very little) or looks plausible (if that's the case, then congratulations!).

Before moving on to phase two to plan your social enterprise, we suggest you complete a concept statement, a simple document that outlines your discoveries from chapters 1 through 7. The concept statement is a short, powerful articulation of the outcome of all the due diligence you have done so far. It is best done in the "canvas" format recently popularized by Alexander Osterwalder,[21] with our version of it shown in this chapter.

The concept statement table summarizes the essence of the problem you wish to attack and the solution you intend to apply to ameliorate the problem. It specifies the market segments you are going after and the criteria by which you will measure your performance, along both social and financial dimensions. It identifies the competition you will be facing and how beneficiaries are going to have to change their behavior in order to benefit from your actions. It specifies the beneficiary experience, the capabilities they require to benefit, and the capabilities you must have for your idea to work. Finally, it pragmatically identifies the sociopolitics the venture will experience and lays out the political strategy you intend to use to address it. Your concept statement can be used to solicit feedback from your advisors and stakeholders. It can also be used to approach investors and other sources of financial support. Table 8.1 provides a framework for creating a concept statement.

Table 8.1: Concept Statement Template

The problem and the proposed solution

1. Problem
2. Proposed solution
3. Required behavioral changes and associated challenges

Business proposition

1. Unit of social impact
2. Unit of revenue

Market and competition

1. Identify market segment.
2. Identify most competitive alternative.
3. State how your solution is better than most competitive alternative.

Sociopolitical landscape

1. Who benefits from my business?
2. Who is hurt by my business?
3. Who are the key stakeholders?
4. Who are my allies?
5. Who are my opponents?

To demonstrate what a concept statement for Zambia Feeds might look like, see Table 8.2.

Table 8.2: Concept Statement for Zambia Feeds

Articulate the problem and proposed solution	
1. Problem:	1. Malnutrition and unemployment in Zambia
2. Proposed solution:	2. Develop an animal feeds business (selling poultry feed) that would open up new markets for subsistence and small-scale farmers, who would then feed their families (addressing malnutrition) and sell fowls in the local markets (earning money).
3. Required behavioral changes and associated challenges:	3. Educate the unemployed in the community about the benefits of raising animals and teach them the entire process of raising and selling chickens.

Business proposition	
1. Unit of social impact:	1. Daily protein serving
2. Unit of revenue:	2. 25 kg bag of animal feed

Market and competition	
1. Identify market segment:	1. Subsistence and small-scale farmers and unemployed people
2. Identify most competitive alternative:	2. High-priced feed producers
3. State how your solution is better than most competitive alternative:	3. Lower-cost, higher-quality feed

Sociopolitical landscape	
1. Who benefits from my business?	1. Local individuals and families
2. Who is hurt by my business?	2. When the business gets big enough, larger competitors in adjacent areas to Copperbelt
3. Who are the key stakeholders?	3. Veterinary board, customers, government (a quality standards board, Zambia's equivalent of the U.S. FDA)
4. Who are my allies?	4. Those our business bought raw materials from, vendors, the customers, and employees of the host company
5. Who are my opponents?	5. When the business gets big enough, bigger existing competitors

Chapter Checklist

Following the processes in this very short chapter, you will have:
- ○ Completed a concept statement.

Tough Love Test

If you answer yes to the following two questions, you are ready to move on to phase two. If you answer no, you have more work to do.

1. Have you and your advisory group put together a concept statement similar to the one in Table 8.2?
2. Do you have consensus that this concept statement appropriately captures the due diligence you have put in to define and design your social enterprise?

From Plausible to Probable: Plan Your Social Enterprise

CHAPTER 9

Frame and Scope the Venture

The first eight chapters of the book guided you through a "due diligence" process to make sure you have really thought through the fundamental business proposition of your venture. It is now time to focus on the operational plausibility of your idea. From here, we will pay a lot more attention to the development of the numbers that will be driving your business. If you're not particularly skilled at number-crunching, this might be a good time to sit down with someone who is and ask them to guide you through the calculations that will indicate whether your project, which makes social impact sense, also makes financial sense.

When we left Ilona at the end of phase one, she had come to the conclusion that her concept for a social enterprise was not only possible but plausible. She had articulated the problem (malnutrition and unemployment), identified a potential solution (start a business selling chicken feed), and settled on a target segment of the market (small-scale or subsistence farmers) that would buy her feed to raise chickens. The next big step for her would be to create a baseline plan to see how the enterprise looks on paper and to determine what she needs to do to meet her revenue and social-impact goals.

Phase two covers the planning process, which will take a concept from plausible to probable. In this chapter and the next two, we will walk through the three steps for creating a discovery-driven plan (DDP) for your social enterprise. The DDP method was developed by Rita Gunther McGrath and Ian MacMillan in their book *The Entrepreneurial Mindset*.[22] Created for use in uncertain business environments, it is a powerful tool for social entrepreneurs. This widely used approach to planning helps managers navigate their way to the real opportunity, or abandon the idea if it is not feasible, at the lowest possible cost.

The core premise behind a DDP is that companies need to be able to plan in a way that maximizes learning and minimizes financial exposure. Rather than creating a plan and obstinately sticking with it no matter what happens, the DDP approach emphasizes learning and redirection as the reality of your situation is made clear, driving down the cost of failure if things don't work out. This approach is crucial in high-uncertainty environments, where it is difficult to anticipate the major challenges you will face. The three key features of a DDP are:

- Framing and scoping (outlined in this chapter)—that is, deciding what are your revenue and social impact goals and determining the resulting scope of operations required to achieve them;
- Identifying operating costs and durable asset costs (covered in chapter 10); and
- Documenting assumptions, creating key checkpoints at which assumptions will be tested, and then continually updating and revisiting assumptions as the project unfolds (chapter 11).

Framing and Scoping the Venture

Social enterprises generally start in highly uncertain environments where very little is known, particularly if you are attempting to create an entirely new market. Here, the DDP becomes indispensable, because you begin with a frame, a clear specification of what you want to achieve annually in terms of social impact and financial performance once the program is running at a steady state, three to five years after start-up. More specifically, you quantify the minimally acceptable social impact target (how many social impact units the project would need to generate) and minimum required financial/funding performance target (how many units of revenue it should make in order for it to be worth the effort). Remember, in chapter 2 you specified the revenue unit and the social impact unit by which you would measure your project performance. For example, "By year five, I want to be reducing the number of diabetes-generated leg amputations by 5% per year and generating profits of $200,000 per year from the ongoing business operation."

It is then possible to reverse-calculate to determine what the revenues, the maximum allowable costs, and the allowable investment in assets must be in order to make these profits. So, while you do not yet know your actual revenues and costs, you can specify what they *need to be* in order for you to make your financial targets. With those numbers, you can back into the scope of operations required to deliver the desired social impact units and revenue units determined in your framing. Ironically, since under near-Knightian conditions you don't know what is going to happen, you have the "luxury" of being able to say what must happen for your idea to be worth the effort. When you frame your project, specify what the social impact and financial outcomes must be, once the venture is up and running, to be worth your while. Once you have framed the required performance, scope the venture by determining how big it needs to be, when it is operating at a steady state, in order for you to make your frame numbers.

The social impact frame and the revenue frame are important for two reasons: First, they are meaningful to you and your organization; second, they are meaningful to the key stakeholders—bankers, investors, potential suppliers—because you need to be seen as capable of delivering sufficient social impact and financial performance to convince these stakeholders that you deserve their support. Remember that other organizations are seeking their support. There are competing demands for the resources your stakeholders will risk by providing funds, skills, and materials to you rather than to alternative resource seekers. For example, if you intend to use a bank for financial assistance, the bank loan officer will need to be convinced that your business can generate enough funds to repay the interest and ultimately pay off the loan. Similarly, suppliers will need to be convinced that it is worth the risk of supplying you with the materials you buy on credit from them. Prospective employees may need to feel convinced that your venture is a superior employment opportunity for them compared to what they are currently doing. Customers such as other businesses will need to have confidence that you will be able to provide a consistent, reliable supply of your offering. Finally, beneficiaries will need to be confident that once they adjust their behaviors to capture your benefits, you will survive and continue to provide those benefits. It is easy to assume that because your product or service is beneficial, beneficiaries must switch from old to desired behaviors, but the perceived longevity of the business plays a big part in their decision to risk switching.

Once you have framed the venture with these objectives, determine what the physical scope of the venture needs to be to make the desired numbers. In other words, how big does the venture need to be in order for you to fulfill your social impact and financial goals? For example, how many widgets do you need to sell, how many people do you need to employ, how many people must be fed, or how many children must be inoculated?

Again, you should complete your DDP based on what should be happening three to five years after start-up, not at start-up. Only if the three-to-five-year targets seem doable should you then go into detailed planning of the launch. If they do not look doable in three to five years, drop the project.

To illustrate framing and scoping, let's start with a simple project: the Khaya Cookie Company case. Then we'll return to the more complicated Zambia Feeds case.

Framing and Scoping: Khaya Cookie Company

Social entrepreneur Alicia Polak came to us several years ago with an idea for an employability project in South Africa. One social statistic that upset her was that in many shantytowns of South Africa, up to 70% of black women who headed households were unemployed. These women typically had as many as five or more dependents (a figure that reflects the growing number of lives lost to HIV/AIDS). Polak saw the situation not as an employment problem, but as an employability problem. The difference is that the unemployable have few skill sets, little or no education, and no work experience. Further, they are trapped in this desperate situation because of their minimal education and absent skills, and are often required to stay at home and care for children. Polak founded Khaya Cookie Company with the main goal of generating employability by developing employee skills through setting up a cookie plant in the middle of Khayelitsha, one of the toughest shantytowns in the province, where women would be trained and employed to make quality cookies for sale outside the township.

Let's look at Polak's framing objectives.

Framing Social Impact: Social Impact Goals

Polak decided she needed to train and employ women, so her unit of social impact was one trained and employable formerly unemployed woman. She wanted to do this for at least 300 women—a number she arrived at after considering the minimum impact she desired to have in order to feel that her efforts and investment were worthwhile. This resulted in the following social impact goal:

> *Social impact goal:* 300 trained and employed women within three years

Note that these goals are often the decision of the social entrepreneur, but we recommend that you and your advisory group carefully consider the aspirations and expectations of key supportive stakeholders identified in chapter 7. In order to mobilize them, they will need to be convinced that the social enterprise is worth their (risky) support.

Framing Financial Impact: Financial Goals

Polak decided that $60,000 per annum was the minimum profit that would justify her forgoing employment alternatives in the region, thus:

> **Financial goals:** $60,000 annual profits after all expenses with a 15% return on sales (ROS)[23] and a 20% return on assets (ROA).[24]

Scoping the Venture Based on the Social Impact Goals

Polak was planning to make gourmet-quality American-style cookies (such as chocolate chip cookies and ginger snaps) and a few other traditional, local types of cookies. After considerable experimentation with local workers over weekends, given the type of product she planned to make and the production system she envisioned, she estimated that one new job would be created for every 800 boxes of cookies she sold per year.*

A job with Khaya Cookie Company, however, was more than just a "job." It was an opportunity to train a formerly unskilled (and therefore unemployable) woman, who could then earn income for her family either by continuing to work at Khaya or by using her newfound skills in other companies nearby.

Alicia's estimate was validated in discussions with local cookie manufacturers. She made it a priority to meet with a number of baked goods producers in order to gather estimates of production capacities, costs, and employment impact prospects. She did so first by identifying a well-known food scientist and consultant who had

---

*This is total job creation: Cookie production requires more than just the person baking. There are employment activities associated with storing, packing, carting, transporting, box assembly, recordkeeping, and so on.

worked with many bakers and knew almost all the bakeries in the region.

Based on her estimates, in order to create 300 jobs, the business would be required to sell 240,000 boxes of cookies annually (300 x 800 = 240,000) into the target market three to five years from start-up.[25] This equates to required monthly sales of 20,000 boxes of cookies. In Table 9.1, the calculation is repeated in tabular form.

Table 9.1: Scoping the Venture—Social Impact Goals for Khaya Cookies

Social impact unit: 1 trained and employed formerly unemployed woman	1
Venture social impact goal: 300 trained and employed women	300
Single employee production capacity (handmade and hand-packed boxes of cookies)	800
Number of cookie box sales required per year to train and employ 300 women	240,000
Required number of boxes of cookies sold per month	20,000

Scoping the Venture Based on the Financial Goals

Polak has set a financial goal of a minimum profit of $60,000 per annum. If the industry net profit margin for premium producers is approximately 15%, then her cookie business must generate $60,000/15% = $400,000 in annual sales. If retailers will pay about $2.00 per box, the required annual number of boxes of cookie sales is $400,000/$2.00 = 200,000 boxes per year. This equates to 16,667 boxes per month. In Table 9.2, the calculation is repeated in tabular form.

Table 9.2: Scoping the Venture—Financial Goals for Khaya Cookies

Revenue unit: 1 box of cookies (sold to customers)	1
Surplus/profit goal	$60,000
Profitability target/performance cushion	15%
Required total sales/annum	$400,000
Estimated wholesale price for a box of cookies	$2.00
Required number of boxes of cookies sold per year	200,000
Required number of boxes of cookies sold per month	16,667

Going through these two calculations gives us two key numbers that determine the actual physical number of boxes needed to be sold to accomplish the business idea. Using these two scoping specifications, Polak can now compare how many boxes of cookies it will take to accomplish her social impact objective with the number of boxes of cookies to accomplish her financial objective.

Social impact scope	Financial scope
20,000 boxes of cookies per month	16,667 boxes of cookies per month

Before she has even sold her first box of cookies, Polak is already getting insight into the necessary scope of the envisioned venture and what the impact might be on revenues and employment. This is worrisome news—if she were to reach her financial goals, she would still not be selling enough cookies to achieve the social impact goal of 300 employees. However, if she can sell enough cookies to employ 300 women, she will comfortably make her financial target.

Note that in Polak's case her social impact scope and her financial scope require similar production quantities. This represents alignment between the desired social impact and her financial aspirations. Such alignment is important—and is useful when you are talking to investors who are interested in supporting only social enterprises with high potential to be financially self-sufficient; for attracting management team members and employees who may be concerned with the long-term viability of your program; and for convincing suppliers and bankers that their participation has sustainable foundation.

Bear in mind also that these are Polak's goals and best estimates of production capacity given her very early research and envisaged methods of production in a highly uncertain environment. As the reality of the situation emerges, so will her expectations. This is okay, as long as she forges a way to meet her minimum requirements. Anything more is a welcome bonus.

Now let's look at the framing and scoping of Zambia Feeds.

Framing and Scoping: Zambia Feeds

This case is more complex than that of Khaya Cookie Company because the entrepreneur, Ilona, is not selling the "end product," namely, chickens. Her business is to sell chicken feed to farmers, who then feed chickens and sell them at market. Thus, her calculations have an added step that Khaya Cookie Company does not.

Framing Social Impact: Social Impact Goals

Remember, Ilona decided that her social impact goal would be to enhance nutrition in her region, specifically protein consumption through increased availability of chicken meat at lower cost, by supplying enough chicken feed to increase regional production of chicken meat by at least 1 million servings per year once the venture was up and running (which was enough for 10,000 people to consume two servings of protein per week).

Social Impact Goal: 1 million protein portions per year

Framing Financial Impact: Financial Goals

A typical bag size for this type of product is 25 kilograms, a weight that is portable on a bicycle or wheelbarrow. Ilona initially chose a 25 kg bag of feed as her revenue unit.

For her time, effort, and entrepreneurial skills, Ilona decided she would generate an annual profit (or surplus for nonprofit companies) of $65,000 per year pre-tax (which would provide after-tax funds of about $45,000)—a suitable but not exorbitant compensation for absorbing the uncertainty of the start-up.

A reasonable pre-tax profit on sales for companies in Zambia was between 10% and 20%, and a reasonable return on assets was between 15% and 25%. Given that poultry production was widely regarded as a high-volume, low-margin business, Ilona decided to shoot for profitability targets of 12.5% ROS and 20% ROA.* Having spoken with bankers and suppliers, she assumed this kind of profitability would be enough to convince them to support her. Bear in mind that these were approximate numbers, taken across industries, and are no more than a start to the plan. In high-uncertainty environments, or those with little available data, it is sometimes necessary to begin with such proxy data simply because there is nothing better with which to start.

Financial Goals: $65,000 pre-tax profits, with a minimum of 12.5% pre-tax ROS and 20% ROA

With these numbers, Ilona could now back into the required scope of the venture.

---

*Bankers and suppliers typically consider at least two measures of performance. The first is profitability, measured by ROS, and the second is ROA.

Scoping the Venture Based on the Social Impact Goals

First, how many 25 kg bags of animal feed will Ilona need to sell per year to ensure that at least 1 million daily protein portions of chicken meat are produced per year?

Discussions with veterinarians and brokers from the poultry industry in South Africa revealed that the optimal weight to sell a live chicken is 4 pounds, and that this yields 8 daily protein portions of edible meat.

To produce 1 million annual portions would require 1,000,000/8 = 125,000 chickens per year, each weighing 4 pounds.

Next, how much feed is needed to grow a 4-pound chicken?

It takes approximately 2 pounds of good-quality feed to yield 1 pound of chicken, so it takes about 8 pounds of feed to grow a 4-pound live chicken.

To grow 125,000 chickens requires 8 (pounds) x 125,000 = 1,000,000 pounds of feed per year.

In Table 9.3, the calculation is repeated in tabular form.

Table 9.3: Scoping the Venture—Social Impact Goals for Zambia Feeds

Social impact unit goal: daily protein servings produced annually	1,000,000
Approximate protein servings per 4 lb. chicken (6–8)	8
Required number of chickens to be sold	125,000
Approximate pounds of feed required per pound of chicken	2
Required pounds of feed to produce per 4 lb. chicken	8
Required feed sales (lbs.) per year	1,000,000
Or U.S. tons per year	500

This is the scope of operations required to achieve the social impact goal. How does this compare with the scope to accomplish the financial goal?

Scoping the Venture Based on the Financial Goals

On checking wholesale prices for feed in Lusaka, the capital of Zambia, Ilona found the average price per ton of feed was $660 for large-scale producers buying in bulk, which meant that for 25 kg of bulk feed, the wholesale price would be about $18. To create a market of small-scale producers, she estimated a price per bag of about $20.

Since Ilona wanted to make at least $65,000 in pre-tax profits, with a ROS of 12.5%, this called for revenues of 65,000/0.125 = $520,000.

This meant that at $20 per bag, to generate the $520,000 revenues, she would need to sell 520,000/20 = 26,000 bags per year.

Converting this number of 25 kg bags per year to tons, this comes to about 717 U.S. tons of feed per year.

In Table 9.4, the calculation is repeated in tabular form.

Table 9.4: Scoping the Venture—Financial Goals for Zambia Feeds

Revenue unit: 25 kg bag of feed (sold to customers)	25
Surplus/pre-tax profit goal	$65,000
Pre-tax profitability target	12.5%
Required total sales	$520,000
Estimated market price for a bag of feed	$20
Required number of feed bags sold	26,000
Required annual sales in U.S. tons (26,000 bags x 25 kg = 650,000 kg at 907 kg/U.S. tons = U.S. tons per year)	717

Going through these two calculations gives us the two key numbers that essentially set up the actual physical activity needed to accomplish the business idea. Using these two scoping specifications, Ilona can now compare what it will take in physical tons per month of feed to accomplish her social impact goal with what it will take in tons to accomplish her financial goal.

Social impact scope	Financial scope
500 U.S. tons per year	717 U.S. tons per year

The number on the left represents the number of U.S. tons of product per year Zambia Feeds will have to sell to make its social impact goals; the number on the right represents the number of tons of product per year Zambia Feeds will have to sell to make its financial goals.

Looking at the two scope numbers, you can see that if Ilona can build a business to achieve her financial goals by selling 717 U.S. tons a year, she will very comfortably make her social impact goal. In fact, she might consider reducing her financial aspirations or increasing the social impact goal to bring about alignment.

This two-scope comparison has three possible outcomes:

1. The numbers are close (we use 10%). This suggests that the two goals are in alignment.

2. The minimum required units of business to make the financial goals are higher than needed (greater than 10% difference) for the benefit desired. This is good news: if the social enterprise can be built to deliver the revenue units, the project will have even higher social impact goals than planned. But the challenge is to configure a business that will actually deliver the target revenue. The closer the plan can be configured to yield the target financial goals, the greater the likelihood of accomplishing the prime goal, which is social impact.

3. The bad news, as in the case of Khaya Cookie Company, is when the minimum required revenue generation units are lower (greater than 10% difference) than those needed for the social impact desired. This suggests that even though you may make your financial goals, your social impact will fall short of what you wanted, which was the purpose of your enterprise in the first place. In cases like this, you may want

to seriously consider either walking away from the project (if you want to preserve the "integrity" of your social impact priority) or compromise and lower the social impact target.

Note that the DDP you will begin to develop to meet this frame and scope looks at the operations you need to put into place three to five years out, when the enterprise is operating at a steady state that delivers the scope you have set, and therefore the social impact and financial goals that make it worth the risk and effort. Only if it looks like you can achieve these conditions should you invest the energy it will take to launch and ramp up operations to that state. For example, in the case of Ilona, her steady-state targets were 717 U.S. tons per year feed production—if she could not meet that, why bother? But clearly she would not hit that production target overnight—it could take at least three years to get there. So her DDP will be built around production levels of 717 U.S. tons per year, and only if it looked doable would she then examine what it would take to start from scratch and build to that production of 700-plus U.S. tons per year.

What Scoping Means to Nonprofits

It may not be typical for a nonprofit to use terms such as *profit* or *surplus*. But even for a nonprofit, it is important to build in a modest surplus of funds over expected costs in order to provide a cushion from unexpected expenses and economic or market shocks. Often nonprofits operating at close to break-even, especially young ones, crumble at the first unexpected setback, increase in expenses, or reduction in funding, which leaves the nonprofit bankrupted and the beneficiaries stranded, sometimes worse off than before. Profit or a planned modest revenue surplus provides a cushion for defense against unexpected adversities. Furthermore, accumulated surpluses can always be used to grow the program once it is more established.

Reality-Checking Your Numbers

In the next chapter, we will take the framing and scoping numbers and start to estimate the costs and revenues associated with all the activities you identified in your Beneficiary Experience and Deliverables tables from chapters 4, 5, and 6. Before doing so, however, look at your framing and scoping figures with a critical eye and ask whether they seem plausible. You can do this through one of the following approaches:

- **Compare your social impact frame with the whole beneficiary population.** If, in your initial calculations, it appears that you will need to deliver your benefits to 50% of the beneficiaries, look at the overall number of potential beneficiaries and ask yourself whether capturing 50% of the "beneficiary market" seems plausible. If your estimates show that you have to sell your product to 5,000 people per month and there are only 10,000 people living in the region, you might want to rethink your sales targets or adjust your expectations.

- **Assess comparable firms.** If there are competing organizations, assess the "beneficiary market share" and capacity of your competition or firms comparable to yours. If your numbers are much greater than theirs, this should be a red flag. You should be able to point with confidence to the powerful advantage your firm will have in comparison with most competitive alternatives.

If, in this process, you find that your initial social and financial goals can't be met, reformulate by revisiting the numbers to come up with a more plausible set of goals—provided, of course, they continue to be worth your while, and attractive to your key stakeholders. Remember that this is just the first step in building a viable learning and execution plan. It is very likely that, in doing your tables, you will already be reformulating your ideas and determining reasonable expectations. This is a normal course of events.

Before proceeding, you should do one more thing: perform another low-cost reality check. Talk to people on the ground—again. Communicate with people living where you plan to launch your venture and ask them to weigh in on the feasibility and acceptability of your project at the scale you are now considering. Elicit their reaction to the following questions:

- What do we absolutely have to do from a legal perspective to operate this scale of business here?
- What is it about our concept at this stage that would cause you alarm?
- What is it about our concept at this stage that would really appeal to you?
- What obstacles do you anticipate we will encounter?
- What similar initiatives have previously failed here and why?

Chapter Checklist

Following the processes outlined in this chapter, you will have:

- ○ Based on the minimum social impact goals you framed, calculated the scope of the business in the form of the physical units of output it will take to meet the social frame, and thought about the plausibility of a business with this scope.
- ○ Based on the minimum financial goals you framed, calculated the scope of the business in the form of the physical units of output it will take to meet the financial goals, and thought about the plausibility of a business with this scope.
- ○ Compared the scopes you calculated from both goals (social and financial) to see if your financial goal can be met while you achieve your social impact goal or better, and adjusted your aspirations if not.
- ○ Run your project by people on the ground to assess its acceptability and ensure it is doable, and identified obstacles you may encounter with implementation.

○ Run your numbers by your advisory group members, asking for any concerns they might have, and heard, if not heeded, their recommendations.

Tough Love Test

If you answer no to any of the following questions, you should seriously reconsider your idea. If you answer no more than once, you should drop the idea. It simply won't be worth your time and resources if you cannot surmount the challenges at this early stage. If you answer yes to all the following questions, by all means, continue on to the next chapter.

1. Are you and your advisors confident that the calculated scope, in the form of physical units of output it will take to meet the social frame, is plausible for your venture?

2. Does the calculated scope of your venture, in the form of physical units of output it will take to meet the financial frame, seem in line with or better than the social scope?

3. Have you run your venture by people on the ground to assess its acceptability, and asked them to identify obstacles you may encounter with implementation and achieving your envisaged scope of operations?

CHAPTER 10

Specify Deliverables

In chapter 6 we introduced the concept of the Deliverables table. This table prompts you to list all major activities that must be completed in order for your venture to be able to deliver the benefits, or social impact, you have in mind. We asked you to consider the types of costs you might incur. Here, we begin to attach some actual numbers to these types of costs. This process will allow you to develop a plan that looks at the cost and revenue flows your venture will generate each year once it is successful. If these cost estimates and performance projections look plausible, begin looking at how to launch your venture. If not, take a step back and invoke your enterprising mind-set to rethink and create a more plausible way to move your enterprise forward.

Calculating Required Revenues, Maximum Allowable Costs, and Maximum Allowable Assets

If you want support from investors, funders, banks, suppliers, and other stakeholders, you will need to have a convincing ROS and ROA. In this section, you'll determine the performance boundaries for your venture by using your framing numbers from chapter 9 to specify what your minimum revenues must be, what maximum costs are allowed, and what the maximum amount of funding (for assets) should be in order to accomplish the profit targets and adequate ROS and ROA targets.

Before we launch into this analysis, we want to share some key ideas for running a disciplined operation. To keep a business sustainable, you need to generate more cash than you spend. There are typically four places where you need to generate surplus cash. Not all four may be relevant to your enterprise, but you should consider which apply and whether there are other potential unanticipated costs.

- **Operating surplus.** You need to bring in more funds than you spend in running the operation. This is pretty straightforward and easy to see—in the case of Ilona, she needs to get more money from her feed business than she lays out for materials, wages, power, rent, maintenance, and so on.
- **Asset replacement surplus.** In the event that you require assets such as machinery, office supplies, IT equipment, and trucks, recognize that these eventually wear out, and you will need to generate enough funds to replace them. To do this, you need to charge yourself proportionate depreciation costs each year, and that is the surplus you need to generate from operations.
- **Inventory and receivables surplus.** If you have a physical product, to protect yourself from the uncertainties and unpredictability of demand for your offering and from delays in supply of your materials, you need to build up raw materials and finished goods inventories—and these require funds. In addition, you will need to set aside funds to absorb the cash flow delays while you wait for your beneficiaries to pay.
- **Debt and investment servicing surplus.** If you are able to, and decide to take out loans, you need to generate additional surplus to cover the interest on them and eventually pay them down. Even if you decide not to take out loans, as altruistic as your investors may be, they will want to see an acceptable return on their investment. (After all, they can always altruistically invest elsewhere.) So, you need to generate enough surplus funds to compete with other seekers of their investment monies.

This may look like grim news, but it explains why so many well-meaning social and charitable enterprises fail. They raise funds from ingenuous donors, launch with enthusiasm and the best intentions, but then run out of funds to operate, to replace, and to absorb fluctuations in demand and supply, and eventually die because they have exhausted donor sources. Sadly, their impact, if they had any, ends up being transient, and they occasionally leave behind beneficiaries saddled with dependency.

You owe it to yourself, your employees, and your beneficiaries to do the relatively simple calculations needed, starting with a specification of performance boundaries: namely, minimum required revenue, maximum allowable costs, and maximum allowable assets. To determine the minimum revenues and the maximum costs and assets, go back to the profit targets and ROS and ROA targets you specified in chapter 9.

Here we return to Khaya Cookie Company to see how this works.

Minimum Performance Requirements: Khaya Cookie Company

The targets for Khaya Cookie were: $60,000 in profits, 15% ROS, and 20% ROA. Using these targets, the performance boundaries for the venture are as follows:

Minimum Performance Requirements: Khaya Cookie Company		
Minimum required revenues	$400,000	Target profit divided by target ROS ($60,000/15%)
Maximum allowable costs	$340,000	Minimum required revenues minus target profit ($400,000 – $60,000)
Maximum allowable assets	$300,000	Target profit divided by target ROA ($60,000/20%)

Minimum Performance Requirements: Zambia Feeds

Remember, the targets for Zambia Feeds were $65,000 in profits, 12.5% ROS, and 20% ROA. Using these targets, the performance boundaries for the venture are as follows:

Minimum Performance Requirements: Zambia Feeds		
Minimum required revenues	$520,000	Target profit divided by target ROS ($65,000/12.5%)
Maximum allowable costs	$455,000	Minimum required revenues minus target profit ($520,000 – $65,000)
Maximum allowable assets	$325,000	Target profit divided by target ROA ($65,000/20%)

Once you have determined the minimum revenues and maximum allowable costs and assets, estimate (from your Deliverables tables) the expected costs and assets. We do this in the next section.

Estimating the Operating Costs

As illustrated in chapter 6, the Deliverables table captures all the operations activities required to deliver your proposed product or service and helps you identify the resources required. In the Deliverables table, we documented the need for equipment, staffing, and materials for each of the steps in the table. So far, we have merely identified the types of costs that would be incurred; the main purpose was to make sure we did not forget an important cost or funding need.

In this section, we will begin to put in estimates for the actual *amounts* of these costs. Keep in mind that at this stage of planning you will not know the exact figure for all potential costs. This is to be expected. You will therefore need to make assumptions about many of these costs, preferably based on field research. However, as long as you do not commit large investments, it is okay to be roughly right rather than precisely wrong. The key point is that you begin to use your assumptions to build the financial proposition of your venture so you can estimate the likely key drivers of cost and performance and the funding that will be required. Greater accuracy will emerge as the venture unfolds and you use your accumulating experience to convert your assumptions to knowledge.

When looking at costs, it is important to recognize that there are two types. First are the ongoing, day-to-day costs of running your enterprise, which are called operating costs. These might include costs such as transporting your goods from your business to your customers, purchasing containers in which to ship your products, paying your employees, or renting your premises. Ideally, these costs will be covered by the income generated by your venture. Second are durable asset costs, which you will likely incur up front. These might include buying equipment and machinery, purchasing land, or building up and keeping inventory.

An easy way to think about these costs is to imagine a car. The car itself would be the fixed, or durable asset, cost, while the gasoline, lubrication, and maintenance would be the operating costs. It's critical that you exhaustively identify both kinds of costs, because they need to be paid out of the revenues from your venture. Note, we almost always suggest that a social entrepreneur first attempt to lease or even borrow any durable asset instead of purchasing it. That way, you will be able to test your venture without having to invest in durable assets, which means a much lower need for (and risk to) start-up funding.

Let's go back to the Zambia Feeds case. In Ilona's Deliverables table (developed in chapter 6), she outlined the *types* of costs she would incur (see Table 10.1 on the following page). Now she has to estimate the approximate costs of these line items, adding columns as in Table 10.2 on page 108 to reflect her estimates. There are two approaches to this. The easier but less reliable approach is to estimate costs as a percentage of revenues, using the percentages of comparable businesses similar to your own. The second is to estimate costs as a cost per unit of revenue, using data you are able to get from the field.

Table 10.1: Deliverables Table Identifying Cost Types for Zambia Feeds

Column A	Column B	Column C	Column D
	Equipment	Staff	Materials
Transportation of raw materials to plant	Trucks	Drivers	
Raw materials storage	Warehouse	Guards	
Raw materials	Warehouse	Guards	Ingredients
Bags	Warehouse	Guards	Bags
Bag Storage	Warehouse	Guards	
Mixing and bagging	Mixing plant, bagging plant	Mixers, baggers	Power
Transportation to distribution center	Truck	Drivers	Fuel
Final mix stored in bags at distribution center			Feed inventory
Administration, financing, overhead, distribution, rent	Office/rent	Office staff	Equipment, supplies

Assigning Costs

As we discussed earlier, in many cases data are hard to come by, if not nonexistent. In this case the only available estimate might be an industry average percentage of revenues (for a nonprofit, an average percentage of budget of similar nonprofits).

In the early estimates for Zambia Feeds, we had to estimate most costs as a percentage of revenues, using data we scrounged from South African poultry operations, from large-scale metropolitan competitors in Zambia, and from U.S. operations—recognizing that the actual numbers would prove to be different.

In the case of raw materials and bags, Ilona was able to determine from her research the cost per ton of feed and cost per bag, instead of assuming these costs as a percentage of revenues.

To calculate the total input cost of a particular type of cost, you need:

- the number of units of input cost per unit of output;
- the cost per unit of that input (we call it the pro rata cost); and
- the total number of output units you will produce.

For instance, if every box of output needs 12 nails, and each nail costs 20 cents (the pro rata cost per unit), and you intend to produce 2,000 boxes, then the total nail cost is:

12 (nails per box) x 0.2 (pro rata dollars per nail) x 2,000 (boxes) = $4,800 nail costs

Similarly, let's say you are going to produce 10-gallon drums of medicine. If every gallon of medicine requires 5 cups of syrup, and syrup costs $2 per cup (the pro rata cost per unit), and you intend to produce 400 10-gallon drums of medicine product, then your syrup costs will be:

10 (gallons) x 5 (cups per gallon) x 2 (pro rata dollars per cup) x 400 (drums of output) = $40,000 syrup costs

Finally, you may not yet have access to fine-grained data and may have to resort to prorating your costs as an estimated percentage of revenues, using cost per unit of revenue proration from similar industries or comparable countries. If every dollar of revenue calls for selling costs of 25%, and you intend to generate $100,000 in revenues, then your first estimate of selling costs would be:

25/100 (pro rata selling cost per dollar revenues) x $100,000 (revenues from output) = $25,000 selling costs

Now let's look at the estimated costs for Zambia Feeds.

Table 10.2: Deliverables for Zambia Feeds —Estimating the Costs

Column A	Column B	Column C	Column D	Column E
	Equipment	Staff	Materials	Estimated pro rata cost/unit*
Transportation of raw materials to plant	Trucks	Drivers		2.0%
Raw materials storage	Warehouse	Guards		1.5%
Raw materials (cost/bag)	Warehouse	Guards	Ingredients	$11.00
Bags	Warehouse	Guards	Bags	$0.50
Mixing and bagging	Mixing plant, bagging plant	Mixers, baggers	Power	10.0%
Finished product storage	Warehouse	Guards		1.5%
Transportation to distribution center	Truck	Drivers	Fuel	2.0%
Final mix stored in bags at distribution center			Feed inventory	1.5%
Administration, financing, overhead, distribution, rent				10.0%

*Examples are per unit sold, percentage of revenues or budget, per month or year, per person, per mile, per ton, per square foot, and so on.

Note: Table 10.2 continues across opposite page.

Column F	Column G	Column H	Column I
Source of estimate	Assumption number	Cost multiplier	Cost estimate (US$)
% of revenues Based of typical Zambian industry cost	1	$520,000 revenues	10,400
% of revenues Based on typical Zambian industry cost	2	$520,000 revenues	7,800
Cost per bag Ilona estimate using South African data	3	26,000	286,000
Cost per bag Suppliers bags	4	26,000	13,000
% of revenues Ilona estimate	6	$520,000	52,000
% of revenues Based on typical Zambian industry cost	5	$520,000 revenues	7,800
% of revenues Based on typical Zambian industry cost	7	$520,000 revenues	10,400
% of revenues Based on typical Zambian industry cost	8	$520,000 revenues	7,800
% of revenues Typical U.S. industry	9	$520,000 revenues	52,000
		Total costs	**$447,200**

To break the chart down:

- Estimated pro rata cost per unit (column E). This represents the pro rata number we will use to multiply the total cost applied to the particular cost being estimated. As you can see, all but two rows are estimates of what these costs will be as percentage of revenue approximations. (Ilona knew specific per-unit costs for bags and raw materials.) Estimating costs as a percentage of revenues is often a necessary first step in moving forward in the absence of better data, subject to validation as your project gets going.

- Source of estimate (column F). If you have no industry data at all, you might just have to make a rough guesstimate, which you should clearly flag as such. All these costs were, in fact, assumptions Ilona was making, and the procedure here is to make assumptions as best you can, then identify the most "dangerous" assumptions (those where the cost of being wrong is the highest). You then need to test the most dangerous assumptions ahead of significant resource commitments, so that if you are wrong, you can bail out before incurring major losses.

- Assumption number (column G). This figure allows you to keep track of your assumptions by assigning a number that flags each one. You will test and recheck these assumptions as the process evolves.

- Cost multiplier and cost estimate (columns H and I). This is where you get around to estimating your costs. In the row devoted to bags, the cost of bags is equal to the price per bag (50 cents from estimated pro rata cost per unit [column E]) times the number of bags needed (26,000 in the cost multiplier [column H], which we gathered from the scope calculation in chapter 9). The cost multiplier is the quantity, or number of units that will be used to deliver the business. When you multiply this quantity by the cost per unit, you obtain the estimated total cost for that cost type. If you are estimating costs as a percent of revenues, you use the total revenues as your quantity: 26,000 bags x pro rata cost per bag of 50 cents = $13,000 as a cost estimate (column I).

Similarly, for raw materials, the estimated cost for ingredients is calculated from the cost per bag of ingredients ($11 in column E) times the total bags to be sold (26,000 in column H) to give a total cost of raw materials of 26,000 x 11 = $286,000. In cases where costs are to be estimated as a percentage of revenues, the cost multiplier we use is the expected revenues. For transportation of raw materials to the plant, the cost of transportation is 2% of revenues (column E), and the cost multiplier we use is total revenues ($520,000 in column H) to give 2% x $520,000 (or $10,400 inserted into column I). The same process is followed for all the other costs, which were estimated as a percentage of revenues.

Now work your way through your own Deliverables table, doing your best to estimate the cost for each of the steps.

Calculating the Total Costs

Adding up all the figures in the cost estimate column (column I) results in the grand total of the estimated costs required to run your business. In the case of Zambia Feeds, the total estimated costs are $447,200.

It's time for the next reality check. With these cost estimates, you need to see whether you are going to achieve your financial goal within the boundaries of minimum revenues and maximum allowable costs just calculated. This is done by putting together an operating income statement using the cost estimated from Table 10.2 (column I).

All you have to do is see whether you will achieve your operating profit (or surplus, in the case of a nonprofit) with the cost estimates you've just made. If it looks like your planned revenues will exceed your costs, and there is a high degree of uncertainty (e.g., there is no similar prior activity in the market), now is a good time to design a low-cost test of your concept with the beneficiaries you have in mind. We offer examples of such tests next. If your planned revenues will not exceed your costs, reconsider your proposed operations model and its associated costs, and begin to think carefully and creatively about how you might do things differently to lower costs to make your venture plausible on paper before you start firing up and burning scarce resources. Once again, an enterprising mind-set is key.

Testing the Concept with Beneficiaries

Referring back to your target segment from chapter 3, you must now select several target customers (at least five) with whom you will test your concept. It is well and good to secure their initial verbal commitment, but this does not mean they will actively adopt your idea or change their behavior when you are ready to enter the market. It is therefore imperative to determine as early as possible whether they will actually commit to your initiative and execute their required activities. In the case of Zambia Feeds, Ilona designed an experiment with a few carefully selected prospects. She recruited two dozen candidates, convinced them to try the poultry rearing program, mixed the first feed batches by hand using part-time workers, and helped the test customers rear the first batches of chickens.

Once these early adopters had succeeded, Ilona tested their commitment further by asking them to buy feed and chicks for the next cycle of production. Only then did she have real evidence that they would pursue the activity—and she was more comfortable in moving forward with her plans. In addition to getting concept validation, Ilona was able to learn more about the beneficiaries, their response to training, and their willingness to follow production guidelines. This was done at low cost, without the purchase of any assets other than a dozen shovels, and with the loan of a shed.

In the case of Khaya Cookie Company, Polak followed a similarly enterprising mind-set. Rather than sign a long-term lease on a baking production facility, she identified an underutilized community building with manifold ovens in a large kitchen and paid a moderate amount on a month-to-month basis to use it. Rather than purchase commercial convection ovens, she first used the smaller domestic ovens that were already there, made several batches of cookies, and secured sales in Cape Town restaurants and hotels.

This mind-set of experimentation and learning is all too often absent in eager entrepreneurs in their early planning and execution phases. However, it is cheaper to spend your imagination before you spend your meager funds in order to learn whether the beneficiaries you have in mind really will view your solution the same way you do. You would be remiss not to consider a time horizon for experimentation. However, this is often easier said than done, as the necessary requirements of one enterprise may vary wildly from another. For example, it is possible to test a poultry growing concept within three to six months, but it may take a full year to develop a prototype software program, and another year to test it in the field. In principle, however, the shorter the time required to concept-test, the better—and we prefer weeks to months for positive evidence of the willingness to adopt a solution by beneficiaries. In the examples just given, the time span to early evidence ranged from 6 months (Zambia Feeds) to 9 months (Khaya Cookie Company).

Now let's return to planning the project and building out the projected income statement.

Projected Operating Income Statement

Now that you have determined the approximate costs and have early proof-of-concept, determine whether you might make the profits you need in order for this business to be financially worth pursuing. In other words, can you generate sufficient operating profits (surplus) to cover your operating costs *plus* the cost of maintaining and replacing any assets such as equipment and buildings, *plus* have enough profits left over to repay loans and repay investors? These latter types of costs are often forgotten by naïve start-ups—at least until the equipment irreparably breaks down or the bank loan officer bangs on the door demanding loan repayment.

Let's start with operating profits. Earlier in the chapter, we calculated the maximum allowable costs. Now we can compare our estimated costs with the maximum allowable costs. If your estimated operating costs are more than the maximum allowable costs, your business is seriously at risk. This means it will not even be able to cover the cost of operations. Even when the allowable costs are greater, there need to be enough operating profits to replace assets that wear down and to repay the loans you took out to buy those assets.

The next exercise serves as a powerful reality check for your venture, and provides the opportunity to assess your proposed venture before committing large amounts of time and resources to an idea that may be seriously at risk. Often, well-intentioned entrepreneurs don't engage in this type of disciplined thinking—they assume their idea is good and that "things will work out"—only to discover later on that they never had a chance of success due to on-the-ground realities and constraints such as limited skills availability, high costs of capital, poor infrastructure, or simply insufficient demand to meet minimum social or revenue targets.

Let's take a look at Ilona's situation, depicted in Table 10.3.

Table 10.3: Zambia Feeds Operating Income Statement

Minimum Performance Requirements: Zambia Feeds		
Minimum required revenues	$520,000	Target profit divided by target ROS ($65,000/12.5%)
Maximum allowable costs (from financial framing)	$455,000	Minimum required revenues minus target profit ($520,000 – $65,000)
Estimated costs (from Deliverables table)	$447,200	

Note: Bear in mind, these are operating costs and that the table doesn't include asset costs and related depreciation costs, interest on loans, or taxes.

Comparing the maximum allowable costs (determined earlier in the chapter) with the estimated costs from the Deliverables table shows that Ilona's estimated costs are already perilously close to her maximum allowable costs. This places her very close to the wind, and vulnerable to unexpected costs or cost escalations.

If the estimated costs had come out even higher—at something like $460,000 to $480,000—we would have pushed Ilona to think about ways of mitigating the two high-cost items: raw materials and mixing and bagging costs. (In fact, it was the high raw materials cost that caused us to begin working with University of Pennsylvania's veterinary school to find ways of mixing the highest-quality feed at the lowest cost.) If she had been unable to do this, we would have encouraged her either to drop the project or perhaps to consider making the venture a not-for-profit with subsidies in the form of grants for operations.

A general rule of thumb here is 20%. Our research tells us that this cushion of at least 20% between maximum allowable costs and estimated costs at this early stage of the planning process is more than likely to be a necessary buffer against underestimated or unanticipated expenses, as well as covering asset replacement and loan repayment. The complete absence of such a cushion should be viewed with alarm.

Estimating the Asset/Investment Requirements

Now let's turn to the kinds of asset costs you will incur and the related funding required for these costs. For the sake of simplicity, we will refer to long-term assets and short-term assets. Long-term, or durable, assets are goods, such as equipment and property, that a firm may have to purchase in order to operate. Short-term assets are assets that have a relatively short lifespan in the company, such as raw materials in inventory, cash on hand for operations, and receivables. Asset costs can be particularly high for those companies producing a product, but even some service companies may need long-term assets, such as trucks and equipment, which need to be replaced as they wear out, or IT equipment, which needs to be replaced when it gets obsolete. You therefore need to be able to cover replacement costs if your venture is to be sustainable. Replacement costs are included in the annual budget as depreciation over the expected lifespan of the long-term asset.

Note that long-term assets should be budgeted for in anticipation of a successful business three to five years out. We *strongly discourage* your purchasing long-term assets at start-up, unless it is *impossible* to borrow, rent, or lease them. All that early purchasing does is deplete your funds and increase the cost of failing if you cannot make your business work. Once your business is up and running, and generating reliable returns, you can consider purchasing long-term assets.

Let's take a look at the Asset Funding table for Zambia Feeds (Table 10.4) on pages 118-119.

To break down the table:

- The Asset Funding table takes the Deliverables table (Table 10.1) as a base and expands it.
- In the "Investment required" (column E), we have simply listed any step in the Deliverables table where funding will be required. For instance, Ilona will have to keep inventory on hand to satisfy unexpected orders from distribution centers, and she may need a truck, if none is available to rent, to deliver product and pick up raw materials.
- In the "Investment amount required" column (F), we list the estimate of the investment needed, and in the "Basis of estimate" column (G), we list the basis of this estimate. For instance, Ilona believes that she will need to have 10 days' inventory as a buffer against delays in supply of materials. This represents 10/365 times sales of $417,000 in inventory, or $11,425 worth of raw materials.
- Ilona's first-cut estimate for the total investment at the bottom

of the "Investment amount required" column (F) is just north of $190,000. Again, since this is an uncertain project, we flag and number all these estimates as assumptions in the "Assumption number" column (H), to be revisited as the plan gets under way and we redirect the project.

- The "Potentially funded by" column (I) lists the sources of funding that Ilona envisages approaching to get her project funded. Note that if the financing costs (such as interest to the banks) for this project are 15%, the total financing costs will be $28,691 ($191,274 x 15%), which must come out of Ilona's $52,000 estimate to cover all administrative, financing, distribution, and overhead costs. This leaves her with only $23,309 ($52,000 – $28,691) for administrative, distribution, and overhead. Again, we would push hard for her to think through how to drive down the investment requirements. Ilona was aware of these costs and managed to eliminate a number of them by starting out as an intrapreneurial venture and persuading her parent firm to absorb costs for the period of start-up. This "piggy-back" strategy allowed her to minimize her overhead and financing expenses until such time as the venture had grown sufficiently to afford them.

With respect to long-term assets, there are two primary considerations: first, the up-front expense of a long-term asset, and second, the replacement or upkeep expense of the asset. Assets must be acquired, appropriately depreciated over time, and ultimately replaced when worn out. The up-front costs must be secured, and the replacement assets planned for. Based on Table 10.4, Ilona will need at least $191,272 to pay for the assets required to operate her venture as planned. Remember that if she secures funding from investors, the investors will require a share of profits. This share must be accounted for ahead of time. If Ilona had raised debt, the interest of the debt would have needed to be paid in a timely manner. This expense would need to have been added to the table.

Table 10.4: Asset Funding Table for Zambia Feeds

Column A	Column B	Column C	Column D	Column E
	Equipment	Staff	Materials	Investment required
Final mix stored in bags at distribution center		Guards	Inventory	Inventory (short-term asset)
Transportation to distribution center	Truck	Drivers		Truck (long-term asset)
Mixing and bagging	Mixing plant, bagging plant	Mixers, baggers	Spare parts, bags	Plant (long-term asset)
Bag storage	Warehouse	Guards		Warehouse (long-term asset)
Raw materials	Warehouse	Guards	Raw materials	Inventory (short-term asset)
Raw materials storage	Warehouse	Guards		Warehouse (long-term asset)
Transportation of raw materials to plant	Trucks	Drivers		Truck (long-term asset)
Finished goods inventory	Bags/warehouse	Guards	Raw materials, bags	Inventory (short-term asset)

Note: Table 10.4 continues across opposite page.

In Ilona's case, there must also be a certain level (as low as possible) of inventory available for customers in the event that they fail to plan well or have a mishap with their feed.

Interpreting the Numbers

Getting to an as-accurate-as-possible projected income statement requires some diligent planning and number crunching. The exercise is well worth it, however, because it is a pragmatic way to assess the viability of your venture *before you commit people and capital.*

Column F	Column G	Column H	Column I
Investment amount required	Basis of estimate	Assumption number	Potential funded by
$11,425	10 days' sales	10	Bank
$12,000	Truck company estimate	11	Investors
$80,000	Ilona's estimate	12	Investors
$5,000	Builder's estimate	13	Investors
$40,000	Ilona's estimate of 10% of revenue	14	Investors/bank
$22,849	20 days' sales	15	Bank
See above: only one truck needed	Ilona's estimate	16	Investors
$20,000	Ilona's estimate of 5% of revenue	17	Investors/bank
TOTAL: $191,274			

This step is really the first time you are comparing your projected revenues with projected costs. Generally, the numbers will put your proposed venture into one of three categories:

- **Viable venture**. Your projected operating costs are 20% less than your projected revenues. (You will make a surplus). This may be a viable venture. But don't get too excited yet; you are still in the very early stages of your venture and there is a lot more testing to be done.

- **Questionable venture**. Your projected operating costs are close to (within 20% of) your projected revenues. It's difficult to make a go/no-go decision here. This scenario is quite common. It is here where we advise that you think creatively (spend your imagination before your funds) about how you might do what is required for less. That's why in the chapter that follows we look at a "sensitivity analysis." This allows you to see which variables you can least afford to be wrong about and which you can afford to overlook temporarily.
- **View-with-concern venture**. Your projected operating costs are close to or greater than projected revenues. In other words, there will be more money going out than coming in. It doesn't take an accountant to realize this is not a good idea. We get really concerned with such ventures, and if you can't innovatively lower costs or increase revenues, then this is not a viable for-profit venture. At this point, you might consider scrapping the idea, or turning it into a nonprofit and bridging the gap with donations and grants. In this way the idea is not lost and there is still a chance to positively affect the beneficiaries for whom the venture was planned.

Chapter Checklist

Following the processes outlined in this chapter, you will have:

- ○ Revisited the Deliverables table for your enterprise, identified the cost drivers of the deliverables required, and estimated the operating costs.
- ○ Established a projected income statement allowing you to compare the projected revenue with the projected costs of running the venture.
- ○ Outlined the costs of maintaining and renewing assets (any durable assets such as trucks or equipment) that will require up-front investment.

○ Identified potential sources of funding for your operations and the acquisition and maintenance of assets.

Tough Love Test

If you answer no to any of the following questions, you should seriously reconsider your idea. If you answer no three times or more, you should drop the idea. It simply won't be worth your time and resources if you cannot surmount the challenges at this early stage. If you answer yes to all the following questions, by all means, continue on to the next chapter.

1. Does your Deliverables table contain a detailed description of all operations requirements necessary to deliver your solution to your beneficiaries?
2. Have you tested your concept with your beneficiaries and received real evidence of their willingness to participate?
3. Is the total of your estimated operating costs at least 20% lower than your calculated maximum allowable costs?
4. Are your estimated operating and asset replacement costs lower than your calculated maximum allowable costs?
5. When the costs of your assets and your funding costs are included in your income statement, are they lower than your projected revenues?
6. Have you discussed your funding aspirations with representatives of the funding sources and received a positive response?

CHAPTER 11

Establish Assumptions and Checkpoints

In the previous chapter, you laid out the expected activities and estimated costs associated with running your business. These estimated numbers are assumptions. Assumptions are simply best-guess estimates that you use perforce until you can test them. In this chapter we offer the procedure you should follow for managing and testing assumptions prior to making large resource commitments in the face of your uncertainty.

At the start of any highly uncertain venture, you simply don't know much about many aspects related to the success you have in mind. Therefore, the assumptions you need to make relative to the knowledge you have are considerable. We call this the assumption-to-knowledge ratio. In DDP, or discovery-driven planning, plan execution is organized around converting highly sensitive assumptions to knowledge as soon as possible, and at the lowest possible cost. This helps ensure that if you are dangerously wrong in your assumptions, you can find out and fix things; or if you can't redirect, you can abandon your plan quickly at low cost. This way, even if uncertainty is high and the probability of potential failure is daunting, the cost of failing is kept low.

Identifying and Documenting Assumptions

The first step is to identify and document, in a consolidated list, all your assumptions. Doing so requires that you revisit the major assumptions you have made so far.

Note that we are not looking here at your initial start-up numbers, but at what you expect (in fact, require) your enterprise to be doing once you have gotten through the initial challenges and are operating at a steady rate—that is, delivering a steady flow of benefits. This could be three to five years after your launch.

Operations Assumptions

You begin with assumptions derived from your Deliverables table in chapter 6. Here are some examples:

- Costs of raw materials and supplies
- Number and types of employees required, and their remuneration costs
- Necessary inventory and receivables (though we strongly discourage receivables)
- Cash required to reach cash break-even
- Preferred profit margins
- Cost of the essential equipment you need
- Cost of maintaining and replacing equipment

To reacquaint yourself with the kinds of assumptions you have made, go back through the earlier chapters where you made and documented estimates about your target market (chapters 2–5), the required capabilities of your beneficiary (chapter 6), your required capabilities (chapter 6), your operational costs (chapter 6), the sociopolitical realities on the ground (chapter 7), and the size and scope of your business (chapter 9).

From these revisits, create a running assumption checklist, updating it as new knowledge becomes available. Examples of assumptions might include pricing estimates from a potential customer, materials or equipment or other input costs provided by a potential supplier, and a labor cost estimate provided by a technician. To get a sense of how this looks, see the simple stylized assumption checklist template in Table 11.1.

Table 11.1: Assumption Checklist Template[26]

Assumption number	Assumption description	Relevant assumption value	Source
1	Market size	Expected number of beneficiaries	Chapter 2 market study/field research
2	Demand	Expected revenues from expected number of beneficiaries	Chapter 2 market study/field research
3	Price	$ (your currency)/unit	Field research/competitors (if any)/preliminary market tests
4	Costs	Materials, labor, equipment, etc.	Field research/secondary research/proxy industry data

The "Assumption description" identifies what you are assuming—for example, the various major costs, the number of beneficiaries, and the price you think you can expect. The "Relevant assumption value" is where you put your current best estimate for the relevant assumption. The "Source" column documents where and when you got or updated the relevant assumption value. A source may be an industry report, a market trial, an expert's estimate, competitive intelligence, or simply your best guess. This column serves as a constant reminder that your assumptions are not facts, but rather, estimates from sources with varying levels of reliability/credibility. Remain vigilant against the tendency over time to forget that assumptions made early on in planning are neither real nor facts. You do not want to learn too late that the actual reality is uncomfortable at best and disastrous at worst.

As you go through this process, and as you begin to uncover new knowledge, you may find yourself redirecting your original plan in order to pursue the actual opportunity emerging from what you are learning. Be aware that a redirected plan may end up quite different from your original concept.

Let's return to the Zambia Feeds case. Ilona soon learned that the assumptions she had made about raw materials reliability, product spoilage, and finance cost had been too optimistic. Her initial estimates proved to be wrong, and in the wrong direction from the actual costs, once she launched the business. Fortunately, by having identified her vulnerability to her assumptions early on, and by developing and baking in disciplined management monitoring processes, she was able to spot these discrepancies and reconfigure her operations and product formulations to reduce the negative impact of emergent outcomes. For instance, having flagged the vulnerability of her profits to raw material costs, she developed a rig-orous purchase inspection process and management practices to monitor and manage the purchase and storage of raw materials, particularly soybeans and corn. After discovering that bags of corn she had purchased contained relatively high levels of sand, she ensured that, thereafter, all soybean and corn purchases would be sampled and checked prior to acceptance. This added an inspection cost to the business but greatly reduced losses due to shipment tampering.

The discovery of flaws in assumptions is a normal consequence of operating in the high-uncertainty environments of social entre-preneurship. The process outlined in this chapter will allow you to identify and monitor those assumptions that matter most to your planned venture.

As your plan evolves, review your original assumptions, seeing where they did not pan out and where and how you should adjust your plan. At this point, go to your advisory group and other knowledgeable people in the field and have them weigh in on your assumptions, then change them if you agree with their advice. The whole idea is to use the assumption table as a tool, both for yourself and to extract advice from experts you respect. Be willing to change your plan while there is still little invested. Do not be defensive about your original plan; under high-uncertainty conditions, most plans change from the original concept.

You need to learn early, and on the cheap, if your idea, or part of it, is not nearly as attractive as you thought it was. If it isn't, abandon it at low effort and low cost. This approach allows you to redirect your efforts and resources to other, more plausible opportunities.

Note the use of "proxy industry data" for assumption number 4 in Table 11.1. You will frequently find it difficult to obtain accurate data for key variables. When this happens, get a rough estimate from a similar, or proxy, industry in another location. For example, when planning her poultry project in Zambia, Ilona used nutrition data from both the U.S. and South African poultry industries, aware that this data was wrong but not an order-of-magnitude wrong.

Alternatively, relevant data from a different industry in the same location—such as drivers' wages in, say, the construction or mining industry—could be a proxy for drivers' wages in food transportation. Use such proxies as a starting point—knowing the data are not accurate but are at least in the ballpark—and refine by testing them as your venture develops.

Identifying the Most Important Assumptions: A Sensitivity Analysis

As you probe and recast your assumptions, it will become clear that some of them are highly uncertain, and therefore difficult or impossible to predict. You and those advising you are likely to be uncomfortable estimating a single value for them. Here you should estimate the *range* of possible values by asking people most in the know to estimate both the worst and the most optimistic values. The more uncertain they are, the greater this range will be. For example, suppliers might estimate that raw materials costs could be as low as $15 in a good year, but as high as $25 in a bad year. Alternatively, your potential banker may not be comfortable suggesting a single foreign exchange rate estimate for a full year. Rather, she might suggest that, in previous years, the rate was as low as 5 to 1 and as high as 7 to 1.

**Table 11.2: Deliverables Table for Zambia Feeds—
Likely and Worst-Case Estimates**

Column A	Column E	Column F	Column G
	Likely pro rata cost estimate*	Source of estimate	Assumption number
Transportation of raw materials to plant	2.0%	% of revenues based on typical Zambia industry cost	1
Raw materials storage	1.5%	% of revenues based on typical Zambia industry cost	2
Raw materials (cost/bag)	$11.00	Ilona estimate using South African data	3
Bags	$0.50	Suppliers	4
Mixing and bagging	10.0%	% of revenues— Ilona estimate	5
Finished product storage	1.5%	% of revenues based on typical Zambia industry cost	6
Transportation to distribution center	2.0%	% of revenues based on typical Zambia industry cost	7
Final mix stored in bags at distribution center	1.5%	% of revenues based on typical Zambia industry cost	8
Administration, financing, overhead, distribution, rent	10.0%	Typical South African industry cost	9

* Examples: per unit sold, percentage of revenues or budget, per month or year, per person, per mile, per ton, per square foot, and so on.

Note: Table 11.2 continues across opposite page.

These ranges allow you to do a sensitivity analysis, which determines your exposure to being wrong for each assumption. Do this by formulating likely and worst-case values for each assumption, then find out which assumptions cause you the greatest exposure to being wrong. Knowing the impact if a worst-case scenario occurs, and its likelihood, can protect you from nasty surprises later on. Also

Column H	Column I	Column J	Column K
Cost multiplier	Cost estimate	Worst-case pro rata cost estimate*	Worst-case cost estimate
$250,000	$10,400	3.5%	$18,200
$520,000	$7,800	2.0%	$10,400
26,000	$286,000	$13,000	$338,000
26,000	$13,000	$0.75	$19,500
$520,000	$52,000	12.0%	$62,400
$520,000	$7,800	2.0%	$10,400
$520,000	$10,400	3.0%	$15,600
$520,000	$7,800	2.0%	$10,400
$520,000	$52,000	12.0%	$62,400

think about what you could do if the worst case happened, and put in place early-indicator signals that it is happening. We'll illustrate the likely and worst-case scenario idea with the Zambia Feeds case (Table 11.2).

We used Deliverables tables from chapter 6 as the basis for this table. We consider the cost estimate (column I in Table 11.2) to be the likely value for each of the assumptions in the spreadsheet. In your version of Table 11.2, add what you believe to be the worst-case values for the assumptions (columns J and K). The worst-case value is the value you currently believe to be the worst possible outcome for that specific assumption, based on the research you have conducted. You now have a range of possible values for each assumption from the likely case to the worst case.

Now let us consider the implications of each assumption on the income statement of Zambia Feeds.

Note that the forecast profit of $72,800 and forecast target profitability (ROS) of 14% both meet the minimums required in the DDP frame in chapter 9 ($65,000 and 12.5%, respectively). Now, in Table 11.3, consider the impact of having the worst case happen for selling price/bag ($18.50) on the profit forecast. This brings profits down to $33,800, which is a reduction of 53.37%. If Ilona discovered that her customers/beneficiaries would pay only $18.50 per bag of feed, the net result would be a 54% reduction in profits, all else being equal. Note also the dramatic effect of raw materials costs: should Ilona discover that raw materials cost $13 per bag rather than $11 per bag, she can expect to see a 71% negative impact on forecast profits, all else being equal. Obviously, she should be deeply concerned about her ability to consistently procure raw materials at a price closer to $11 per bag (or less).

In the Zambia Feeds example, Ilona is able to rank the assumptions according to impact on outcome, thereby focusing on only those few assumptions that have greatest impact on her venture. This allows her to ignore, for the time being, the (many more) relatively less important variables. Therefore, her assumptions priorities would be ordered:

1. Raw materials (cost/bag)
2. Selling price/bag
3. Mixing and bagging
4. Administration, financing, overhead, distribution, rent
5. Transportation of raw materials to plant

Table 11.3: Zambia Feeds Project

Required operating income	$65,000
Target number daily protein servings	1,000,000
Target profitability (ROS)	12.5%
Required revenues	$520,000
Allowable costs	$455,000
Estimated selling price/bag	$20.00
Required bags of feed sold	26,000

Deliverables specification/ assumptions	A Likely cost estimate	B Worst case	C Profit (US$)	D Profit (%)	E Impact rank
			Worst-case impact on		
Selling price/bag	$20.00	$18.50	$33,800	-53.57%	2
Transportation of raw materials to plant	$10,400	$18,200	$65,000	-10.71%	5
Raw materials storage	$7,800	$10,400	$70,200	-3.57%	8
Raw materials	$286,000	$338,000	$20,800	-71.43%	1
Bags	$13,000	$19,500	$66,300	-8.93%	6
Mixing and bagging	$52,000	$62,400	$62,400	-14.29%	3
Finished product storage	$7,800	$10,400	$70,200	-3.57%	8
Transportation to distribution center	$10,400	$15,600	$67,600	-7.14%	7
Final mix stored in bags at distribution center	$7,800	$10,400	$70,200	-3.57%	8
Administration, financing, overhead, distribution, rent	$52,000	$62,400	$62,400	-14.29%	3
TOTAL ESTIMATED COSTS	$447,200				
FORECAST PROFIT	$72,800				

Conduct this exercise for each of the assumptions for your venture and rank each assumption in order of its impact on your venture. Typically about five to eight of your worst-case assumptions will have a huge negative impact on performance; most of the others will have only limited impact. In fact, if you have more than eight high-impact assumptions, we would be seriously worried about the vulnerability of your venture.

Though it is a little tedious to do the worst-case calculations in a spreadsheet, it is a lot better than being sideswiped in real life. No one wants to fail after having poured in huge effort and serious investment. As your venture unfolds and the accuracy of your assumptions becomes clearer, use your calculator or spreadsheet to systematically update your plan and identify the assumptions that matter most.

You can also do sensitivity analyses using more sophisticated methods, such as Monte Carlo simulations. Once you have conducted your sensitivity analysis (manually or using Excel Solver or a Monte Carlo analysis), you will know which assumptions are likely to have the most impact on your proposed business model. You can therefore decide which to test first. Do this by designing and then using a sequence of checkpoints as laid out in the next section.

Designing Checkpoints to Test the Most Sensitive Assumptions

Checkpoints are progress points or events that you deliberately design to test the most sensitive assumptions in your business plan. Types of checkpoints range from doing market and feasibility studies, to launching small pilot programs, to building a model or prototype. Checkpoints are important because they force you systematically to test and learn about critical assumptions before committing significant resources. They also help ensure that you do not treat assumptions as facts. Be warned: treating assumptions as facts happens more frequently than you imagine—sometimes with catastrophic effects.

Designing Checkpoints

To develop a set of checkpoints, first think about ways to test your assumptions at major events in preparation for and during the launch and growth of your project. Start with the high-impact assumptions from your sensitivity analysis. Once you have identified them, think of checkpoints (such as market studies, feasibility analyses, or pilot programs) where you can begin to test these key assumptions. For the high-impact assumptions, you should have multiple checkpoints, starting perhaps with inexpensive, rough-and-ready tests. Then, as you reduce the uncertainty of your assumptions and increase confidence, you "earn" the right to spend more in order to get better estimates of the value of the assumptions.

Different types of businesses will have different checkpoints. Tables 11.4 and 11.5 on the following pages contain typical checkpoint templates for a manufacturing business (11.4) versus a service business (11.5).[27] Further on in the chapter, we will look at project-specific examples.

The goal in designing checkpoints is to obtain the most information for the least amount of money. For example, if you are a software developer, it makes more sense (and is significantly less expensive) to use rapid prototyping to test usability by putting "friendly" users in front of a prototype with modest functionality, than to fully build out the software before putting it in front of hard-nosed customers or investors.

In the first part of this chapter, we introduced the idea of developing a list of assumptions. We then talked about how to identify key assumptions—those that can make or break your business. Now you need to decide at which checkpoints you will test (and retest) your key assumptions, and enter them into the most important

Table 11.4: Checkpoint Template for a Manufacturing Business

Checkpoint	Assumption tested
Industry analysis and market study completed	Price, market size, and demand potential
Feasibility study done	Operating costs (rental, power, etc.), potential returns
Prototype developed	Costs, resource availability, development time frame
Initial customer test with focus groups completed	Price, product feature demand
Trials with beta users performed	Price, demand cycle
Pilot plant completed	Capital, raw materials, equipment, labor costs
Pilot marketing campaign completed	Price, demand, customer-acquisition costs
Pilot sales recruitment and training done	Labor availability, compensation cost
Manufacturing recruitment and training done	Labor availability, compensation cost
Plant commissioned	Operating costs, productivity
Sales force recruited and trained	Labor availability, compensation cost
Product launched	Price, key operating costs, customer demand
Initial orders received	Price, customer demand, selling costs
First returns received	Quality, customer segment needs

planning document: a Checkpoints and Assumptions table. The goal here is to have one table that specifies which assumptions will be tested at which checkpoint—keeping in mind that very important assumptions will be tested more than once.

If you look at our sample Checkpoints and Assumptions table (Table 11.6 on page 136), you will see that every checkpoint tests at least one assumption, and every assumption is tested at least once. You never want to reach a checkpoint and have no assumptions to test—why have the checkpoint? Similarly, you never want to

Table 11.5: Checkpoint Template for a Service Business

Checkpoint	Assumption tested
Industry analysis and market study done	Price, market size, and demand potential; competitor pricing
Feasibility study done	Operating costs (rental, power, etc.), potential returns
Mock-up system or rapid prototype developed	Labor costs, development time frame
Initial focus groups on mock-up system testing completed	Price, service features, demand
Human resource and manpower study done	Skills availability, costs
Trials with beta users carried out	Price, key features, demand
Pilot system development done	Costs, development time frame, key skills availability
Test operating system developed	Customer demand, operations costs
Pilot sales recruited and trained	Skills availability, training costs, compensation
System tested with beta users	Service features and costs
Sales and operations staff recruited and trained	Labor costs, skills availability
Initial contracts signed	Price, sales cycle, selling costs, demand
Service launched	Price, operating costs, sales cycle, demand

have an assumption that is not tested at least once, or you run the risk of being very expensively wrong about that assumption. This is absolutely crucial in high-uncertainty environments where a forgotten assumption such as "market demand" or "transport cost" can prove to be the death of a well-intentioned venture.

Always design your Checkpoints and Assumptions table so that the most sensitive, "showstopper" assumptions are tested earlier than less sensitive assumptions and tested more than once.

In addition to the most sensitive, showstopper type of assumption is a hypercritical type of assumption we call the go/no-go assumption. It is similar to a showstopper, but different in that if you are wrong about it, it will preclude your launching your venture at all or halt it suddenly and unexpectedly. For example, if Khaya Cookie Company could not get approval from the U.S. Food and Drug Administration (FDA), it would be unable to sell in the U.S. market, regardless of the quality of its product or the appeal of its packaging.

Often, go/no-go assumptions are regulatory or legal in nature, such as work permits for key employees or a license to operate. Try to resolve go/no-go issues before you incur substantial expenses and/or have customers expecting deliveries only to have their orders held up by the authorities.

Now let's look at an example of the Zambia Feeds project's checkpoints and assumptions in Table 11.6.

At checkpoints A, B, and C, Ilona called and visited farmers, vendors, and local markets to get a sense of the prices chickens were being sold for and the costs of rearing them. This provided her with

Table 11.6: Zambia Feeds Checkpoints and Assumptions

	Checkpoint	Assumption tested
A	Historical poultry price analysis report complete, historical mixed feed sales report completed	Market price
B	Historical price analysis report complete, historical raw materials prices report completed	Feed cost
C	Cost/price financial model completed	Market price, feed cost, site rental, labor estimates, transportation estimates
D	Hand-mixed feed *sample* shipment sent to test region	Market price, feed costs, transportation costs
F	Bulk hand-mixing pilot phase completed	Market price, feed costs, labor costs, delivery costs

fundamental insights into what it would take for small-scale farmers to rear poultry and sell the chickens at local markets.

At checkpoint D, Ilona hired six part-time workers to mix feed by hand on a concrete floor inside a shed. The mixed and bagged product was delivered to customers in the test region. They, in turn, reared and sold their chickens. By means of a profit-share incentive with the parent firm, Ilona negotiated free use of the shed until there was sufficient evidence that the business could be scaled. Once the key assumptions of market price, feed costs, and labor costs had been approximately validated she was able to continue with her venture.

At checkpoint E, Ilona convinced two dozen individuals in nearby villages to spend six weeks rearing a batch of chicks, which she supplied. In exchange for their investment commitment— early farmers used savings or borrowed funds—she guaranteed them sufficient feed and consulting assistance during the growing cycle. Once the chickens reached maturity at six weeks, the farmers transported them to the local cash market and were delighted to receive a healthy profit of nearly $1.00 per bird. Ilona had thereby tested a bigger "bulk" production run and gathered more information on market prices and feed costs. Notice the pattern of learning at low expense and the subsequent commitment to larger venture investments only when important assumptions are converted to knowledge.

The Checkpoint Review Process

As your venture progresses, you will need to refine your assumptions by deliberately testing and improving them at the major checkpoints you set up. The first step in this process is to list all the assumptions you have made so far. Armed with this list, begin eliciting reactions from people knowledgeable about similar markets, products, factory owners, retailers, etc., asking them to weigh in on the reasonableness of your assumptions; or by calling potential customers or suppliers and probing them for their reactions. If anyone expresses concern, find out why. Ask them to suggest alternatives, and their reasoning behind their alternatives. Often just a few phone calls or personal discussions with potential beneficiaries, distributors, suppliers, or industry experts can provide critical information about your assumptions. These kinds of informational checks cost little and can prevent huge, costly errors.

At each checkpoint, discuss with your advisory group what you have learned and the extent to which you need to revise your venture. Ask questions such as:

- What did we originally hope to achieve at this checkpoint and what actually happened?
- Why did it happen and what have we learned?
- Do we need to redesign our offering? Can the objectives be accomplished or should we revise them?
- Have new opportunities been uncovered?
- What do we need to test at the next checkpoint, and what funding and time will it take to move to the next checkpoint?
- Important: each checkpoint, revisit your Stakeholder Impact table from chapter 7 and see how it has changed. If it has meaningfully done so, revisit your sociopolitical strategy and update your Tactics table (discussed in chapter 7).

Moving On

If, after testing your key assumptions, your idea continues to have positive prospects, move on to the formal launch and piloting phase: phase three. This will take your project from probable to plannable. We view a pilot as the first on-the-ground practical test of a business case. Be as parsimonious as possible with your pilot. With imagination, pilots can often be done cheaply and quickly. For instance, don't build an entire school when you can rent a room and start a pilot course with just one class of students.

In the case of Khaya Cookie Company, Polak negotiated the use of an unoccupied community building with a large kitchen with idle ovens, rather than buy a building and bakery equipment. As we saw, Ilona first hand-mixed the feeds by means of a shovel team rather than buying mixing equipment; later, she used secondhand equipment before buying new equipment.

With your Checkpoints and Assumptions table fleshed out, now turn to phase three and begin to pilot your venture.

Chapter Checklist

Following the processes outlined in this chapter, you will have:
- Identified and documented your assumptions.
- Identified the assumptions that have the greatest impact on your venture.
- Developed a Checkpoints and Assumptions table designed to test no more than 10 most important assumptions.
- Structured your checkpoints in keeping with the philosophy of learning at low expense (converting assumptions to knowledge) before committing to large investments.
- Made sure you have a process for updating your Stakeholder Impact table and modifying your Tactics table, which was discussed in chapter 7, in the face of unfolding sociopolitical realities.

Tough Love Test

If you answer no to any of the following questions, you should seriously reconsider your idea. If you answer no three times or more, you should drop the idea. It simply won't be worth your time and resources if you cannot surmount the challenges at this early stage. If you answer yes to all the questions, by all means, continue on to phase three.

1. Does your list of assumptions contain a clear description of *all*

currently known assumptions necessary to deliver your solution to its beneficiaries? Has this been affirmed by your advisors?

2. Have you identified the most sensitive assumptions, the ones that give you maximum vulnerability?

3. Have you designed a Checkpoints and Assumptions table, initially with no more than five checkpoints, designed to test the 10 most import-ant assumptions? Does it comply with the mantra of "investing a little to learn a lot"?

4. Have you come up with the lowest possible cost means to roughly validate your most important assumptions—in other words, are you working on inexpensive ways of being roughly right rather than expensive ways of being precisely wrong?

5. Do you have a process for ensuring that you revisit and update your Stakeholder Impact table at each checkpoint? Is it necessary to update your sociopolitical strategy? Does your updated sociopolitical strategy reflect the current realities, and are you confident that you can manage the sociopolitics?

From Probable to Plannable: Launch and Scale Your Social Enterprise

CHAPTER 12

Launch Your Enterprise

In phase one, you took your start-up idea from possible to plausible, and pressure-tested it. You selected your initial target market segment and formed an advisory group for your venture. In phase two, you took your venture from plausible to probable, and created a DDP, or discovery-driven plan. Then you identified the most sensitive assumptions in your plan, and designed a systematic method of testing them at predetermined checkpoints. You now have done all the due diligence needed to move to phase three and take your venture from probable to plannable. Your venture is ready for a controlled launch.

A controlled launch is the formal initiation of commercial enterprise operations, in a way that:

- Prioritizes learning ahead of investment,
- Minimizes initial investments and costs,
- Postpones the acquisition of assets for as long as possible, and
- Allows for project redirection as you learn more about on-the-ground realities.

There's some inevitable repetition from prior chapters in the first section of this chapter. This is because the process of forging opportunity out of uncertainty is iterative and cyclical, driven by intelligent experimentation and deliberate learning.

Preparing the Ground

In order to get your project off the ground, we will walk you through two key preparative procedures: identifying the skills you need and thinking about how to minimize your early investment to minimize risk. Let's start with identifying skills.

Skill-up for Start-up

First, make sure you have the staffing to launch your enterprise. We don't mean assembling a vast number of people, but, perhaps initially, on a part-time basis, enough people with the skills that are absolutely essential to get your new enterprise started. In our experience, at least four skills are needed to get an enterprise going:

- **Selling skills.** Make sure at least one member of your team is skilled at securing sales. The type of sale that needs to be made is not simply order taking, but convincing (perhaps) dubious purchasers that your offer is worth their risk and support. Any new enterprise is a risky business at best, and potential supporters—such as customers or beneficiaries, potential allies, and needed indifferents from your stakeholder analysis—can be forgiven for being circumspect about supporting something entirely new. You will need at least one person on your team who is effective at persuading prospective supporters. The salesperson should be deeply aware of the perceived risks—in the minds of the potential customer or beneficiary—and be able to think of ways to help the beneficiaries risk making those critical first few orders. A smart "missionary" salesperson is able to find ways of underwriting the perceived risk for that seed beneficiary. If you do not have someone capable of securing essential support for your enterprise, you will struggle to make those sales, and thus will generate no revenues, and the project will be hampered, if not doomed, from the start. You may need to lean on your advisory board to help you find somebody who can secure those sales or help you do it yourself.
- **Operating skills.** The ability to manage operations—with particular emphasis on meeting schedules and planning—and maintain quality of your output is crucial. You need somebody

to take charge of operations, someone who can pay attention to detail and make absolutely sure that everything—from the ordering of materials through the production of product through the storage of finished goods—is tightly under control and not a target of pilfering or sloppy work leading to low-quality products. This kind of talent is often scarce and expensive. You may need to budget money and time to train and develop suitable staff.

- **Accounting and cash flow management skills.** Cash flow crises are prime killers of start-ups, and almost every new enterprise comes under intense cash flow pressure. In fact, even an enterprise that is doing very well and growing can quickly experience cash flow pressures because of the need to build inventory and receivables ahead of growing demand. Be sure that there is someone on your team capable of and responsible for monitoring and managing cash flow.

- **Negotiating skills.** In our experience, for every new enterprise, there are between three and five mission-critical negotiations whose outcomes will fundamentally imprint the success of the enterprise. If the negotiator does a bad job, it will cripple your performance for a long, long time. Prior to the launch, review your Deliverables table to identify the most critical negotiations on the horizon—ones where you'll have to cut a feasible deal for the operation to work at all. Let's look at negotiation challenges in more detail next.

Three Negotiation Challenges

A successful launch depends on negotiation outcomes. There are three key challenges.

- **If the negotiation does not work, your enterprise dies and the other party goes on to do business with others like you.** In a social entrepreneurship venture, you are unusually dependent on cutting a deal in which you are confident the deal will be executed.

- **You are negotiating from a position of weakness.** Spend some time thinking through what you absolutely *must* get from the negotiation for it to be worth your while. When you are in a position of weakness, you have some really tough decisions to make. First, think about what we call your "walkaway position." Decide the worst possible deal that you can accept. Go into the negotiation with a clear line in your mind. If it's crossed, walk away. If you do not enter the negotiation with a clear idea of your walkaway position, you will find yourself conceding way beyond what makes sense from a business point of view. In the heat of negotiations, and under pressure to get a critical deal done, there is an enormous temptation to accept whatever offer is being made and then just hope against hope that that "things will work out." Believe us, things will not work out.

- **Prepare for what could go wrong with the execution of the deal.** Your initial due diligence and advisory group discussions will have put you in a stronger position to do this. Now use what you have learned to bake into the deal agreements on how the deal will be executed, by whom, and when, and what happens afterward. Do all you can to ensure that both parties are clear on all the actions and activities each will carry out to uphold its part of the deal. Take the example of Zambia Feeds: if your customers are waiting for batches of chicks to be delivered to their farms, and something goes wrong with the delivery, it is too late now, while the feed is spoiling, to start arguing about what the deal was with respect to delivery and timing, including penalties for nonperformance.

Important, and related to this problem, is that in many cases your start-up venture is of relatively low priority to other, more established stakeholders, so in times of stress they will have no compunction about making you wait while they pay attention to bigger and longer-tenured customers.

In your key negotiations, it is not just a matter of negotiating what prices you will pay; you need to reach ex ante agreements on what specifically happens when one party fails to execute, how to measure compliance with agreement, and who is going to take responsibility for what action if the terms of the contract are not met.

Minimize Early Investment

As you launch your enterprise, you need to be obsessive about minimizing early investment and managing cash outflows. The person responsible (you or one of your managers/employees) needs to be fully on top of cash flow and cash flow projections. In your launch phase, make sure you have done everything possible to avoid laying out cash before cash comes in. Make sure you don't buy assets when there's not a revenue stream to justify their purchase, or incur high fixed costs when there's not enough revenue to justify such costs.

Here are some simple rules to help you minimize initial investment:

- **Don't buy equipment if you can rent or lease (or even borrow) it.** Remember, Ilona started her business in a shed with a concrete floor, and with shovels, not with brand-new production equipment.
- **Subcontract production or import products initially, even though it costs more per unit.** This saves you having to fund your own production assets or service delivery system until you have unit sales great enough to justify building a complete production system. Buy your own plant only when it is evident that you can generate sufficient sales to justify such a purchase.
- **Don't take on full-time staff, especially relatively expensive managers.** Wait until you have evidence that they will be able to generate the revenues you need to cover their cost. Until you have reliable cash inflows, pay per task completed as opposed to paying a fixed income.

- **Minimize working capital.** Building inventories and receivables ties up cash. Try to secure longer times to pay vendors. Avoid or minimize selling on credit; this sucks up cash and, furthermore, exposes you to collection risk.
- **As the business gets started, make sure your team knows the current daily and weekly break-even sales.** For example, if weekly break-even sales are 100 units, and by Wednesday your sales are only 40 units, your salespeople know they have to get out and sell 60 units by Friday. If your break-even sales are 20 per day, and by Friday your operations has produced only 85 units of adequate quality, everyone knows they will be working through the weekend. Yes, the weekend.

Hitting the Start Button

Once you have skilled up, and found ways to minimize your early investment, you are ready to launch.

Specify Your Key Initial Beneficiaries: "Naming Your First Five Customers"

Think carefully about the characteristics of the first few beneficiaries you will sign on. Like an infant in the first few months of life, your newborn enterprise will undergo critical early learning. Spend some time thinking carefully about who should be the "first five" customers. After all, you cannot sell 1,000 units until you have sold the first 100, and you cannot sell your first 100 units until you have sold five! And it is those first five that are the seeds of the future business.

We spend time specifying the customers and customer context of the first five sales. Who are the important seed beneficiaries in your target segment? Describe those first few sales using the guidelines that schools of journalism provide to budding journalists. An article is incomplete unless it answers six key questions: who, what, where, when, why, and how.

- **Who is going to buy?** Describe your expectations as to your buyers' characteristics: age, gender, education, and any other key traits that capture the essence of who you think will be your very first beneficiaries.
- **What are they going to buy?** Here the challenge is to get into the beneficiary's head and specify, along the lines espoused by Clayton Christensen and colleagues,[28] what the "job" you're offering is going to do for the beneficiaries that would cause them to "employ" your product or service rather than something else with their extremely limited funds?
- **Where are they going to buy?** Describe where you think the sale will take place.
- **When are they going to buy?** Describe when you think the sales will take place, and with what frequency.
- **Why are they going to buy from you?** Describe why you think they're going to buy from you and not choose the most competitive alternative.
- **How are they going to buy?** Describe what behavior patterns they will follow in making the purchase, and how big their order will be.

We ask you to do this because when an actual sale takes place, you can make a detailed comparison of where the transaction resembles or differs from your expectations, and perhaps adjust your selling to take into account the new realities. Each sale you make early on is an opportunity to consciously and rapidly learn about your true customer base and the actual selling conditions. In addition, it each enables you to redirect your venture if it looks like your early assumptions were incorrect.

Do yourself a favor by taking the time to assess your first ten or so beneficiaries by filling out an Expectations vs. Actual Results table (see Table 12.1), then look at any major differences between your expectations and the actual results of your marketing efforts.

Table 12.1: Expectations vs. Actual Results for Zambia Feeds Launch

Expected result	What	Who	When
	Quality birds	Villager	Monthly
Actual result			
Beneficiary 1: Small-scale rural villager	• Protein for family • Means of generating income	• Small-scale rural villager	• Bimonthly/ each bird cycle
Beneficiary 2: Small-scale peri-urban grower	• Product performance • Quality birds • Income generation	• Small-scale peri-urban grower	• Bimonthly/ each bird cycle
Beneficiary 3: Medium-scale commercial	• Product performance • Quality birds	• Commercial grower	• Monthly

Note: Table 12.1 continues across opposite page.

Note the differences among the beneficiary/customer types in Table 12.1. For Beneficiary 1, the small-scale rural villager, it soon became apparent that the transportation costs of getting feed to the beneficiary and the birds to market were too high, thereby compromising beneficiary self-sufficiency. In other words, for Beneficiary 1 there was simply not enough profit in the production of a bird to cover the cost of feed and the total cost of transportation. This led to Ilona's first redirection of Zambia Feeds toward the small-scale peri-urban grower, extended later on, to the medium-scale commercial grower.

With respect to small-scale peri-urban growers, an eight-week shelf life was found to be insufficient as these customers could afford to buy feed only once per production cycle (eight weeks) due to the fact that sometimes the feed was in the distribution system for two

Where	Why	How
Distribution center/ agent outlet	Sell birds	Self-transport
• Distribution center • Agent outlet	• Only feed available rurally • Zambia Feeds consulting support • Zambia Feeds–supplied chicks	• Bicycle • Minibus taxi
• Distribution center • Agent outlet	• Quality of product • Technical support	• Bicycle • Minibus taxi
• Delivered by Zambia Feeds if road accessible (minimum 3 tons)	• Quality of product • Consistency and availability	• Self-collection • Zambia Feeds

to four weeks. So Ilona had to modify her feed formulas to meet a three-month shelf life requirement to accommodate the buying patterns of that particular beneficiary segment.

This exercise also proved to be powerfully beneficial to Jaytee's venture, AidsAid. That business observed the reactions of nurses and patients to early graphic user interface (GUI) graphs. The team's early expectations were that the EMR system would be most useful for patient data management, research, and clinical decision-making. However, once patients saw, in graphic format, the relationship between treatment adherence and their physical health, they began to request to see their charts at each visit. Physicians and nurses discovered that they could more easily persuade patients to adhere to treatment regimens with the aid of patient charts. This was a powerful development; however, it was neither predicted nor planned for.

Relentlessly Deliver Quality

You will almost always have quality problems at the very start, which means rework, with the associated higher-than-expected production costs.

A common mistake is for social entrepreneurship start-ups, in desperation, to fall prey to the urge to ship out poor-quality product, especially under cash flow pressure, when the unexpected costs arising from discarding poor quality offerings poses an enormous temptation not to do so.

If your initial sales are unreliable or of low quality in the eyes of those pioneer customers "brave" enough to sign up with you, your business will be compromised. You need somebody on board making sure the products or services you deliver are seen by beneficiaries as timely and of high quality. Only this will assuage any concerns beneficiaries about the riskiness of doing business with you, and they can then perhaps even be used as endorsers.

Doing something new to the world or new to a particular market is a serious challenge. Without a firm idea of what constitutes quality in this area, it behooves the person responsible for operations to spend time with beneficiaries, who can help flesh out the criteria by which the quality of your offering will be judged. Then make sure your enterprise delivers that quality, and that beneficiaries acknowledge this.

Celebrate Early Successes

If you are having difficulty securing early transactions with beneficiaries or when the going gets tough in general, even small successes are heartening. It pays to go for early "quick hits." Even if they are relatively small, they demonstrate that progress is being made. Examples of quick hits are trial orders by beneficiaries, validated prices, met cost targets, shipment of the first few orders, declarations of support by influential members of the community—anything that can be seen as evidence that your venture is working. Do whatever you can to secure early evidence of success, or else run the risk of morale declining. Then broadcast it within the organization, reward the responsible employees, and seek out the next win.

Aggressively Use Your Checkpoints and Assumptions Table

As your venture gains momentum, continue to use your Checkpoints and Assumptions table. Here are some tips:

- **Appoint someone (even yourself) as "keeper of the assumptions."** This person's formal responsibility will be to track the assumptions and test them at every designated checkpoint. This is important. We all get busy, the checkpoints slip by, and inadequate or flawed assumptions slip by with them—then expensive corrective action must be taken. The most sensitive assumptions in particular should be tested. If it turns out that the project is off track, get together and replan.
- **Pressure test learning.** As the project unfolds from checkpoint to checkpoint, if you find evidence that a critical assumption will not pan out, a powerful way to pressure-test your key assumption is to design a test to show it is wrong, rather than trying to prove it right. This is psychologically tough to do, but if you can find inexpensive and early evidence that the business just won't fly because some assumptions are off track, you avoid excessive and unnecessary waste of effort and resources. In one project, peanut farming by villagers in Malawi, we disengaged very early on because of the cost to transport the peanuts from rural Malawi to processors in South Africa. The proponents of the project had suggested that the export market would be feasible and attractive under the right conditions. Our DDP indicated an absolute maximum transportation cost that the business could profitably bear. As our first pressure test of the proposal, we thoroughly investigated all possible transportation alternatives,

to show that the absolute minimum cost would exceed the deal-killer maximum allowed. All that it cost us was the time to do the DDP and a few lunch meetings with highly knowledgeable freight forwarders.

- **Treat early sales as inexpensive learning opportunities, not as required revenues.** In uncertain environments, your first offering in the market should be seen as a sacrificial, or "trainer," product—a tool to learn about the intended beneficiaries and the relevant context. For example, programmers use rapid prototypes of software applications as trainer products to develop the application further based on user feedback. In the AidsAid project, our rapid prototyping beta software version was a basic EMR system run off a server hosted locally. As additional user requirements (such as electronic reporting and graph generation) emerged, the application was built out. In this way, our further development was better informed than if the programmers had tried to guess up front what the clinic would want and be prepared to pay for.

- **Use after-action reviews.** When there are major disconnects between your DDP and what actually happened at a checkpoint, there is a need for redirection. Every redirection is an opportunity to learn from the past what to do better in the future. One way of doing this is to conduct an after-action review, which is a structured review that analyzes the project to understand what happened and why, and to determine what can be done better.

Regularly Update Your Discovery-Driven Plan and Stakeholder Impact Table

Applying the principles in this chapter should have you on the road to the steady state condition you planned for in your DDP. However, in the throes of activity in which you find yourself during a launch, it is all too easy to fail to revisit and update your DDP and stay abreast of what is happening with your stakeholders. This is why it is important to have the formal "keeper of the assumptions" to update the Checkpoints and Assumptions table and revisit the Stakeholder Impact table at each checkpoint.

Chapter Checklist

After completing the processes outlined in this chapter, you will be doing or will have done the following:

- Ensured you have access to the key skills you'll need to start: sales, operations, financial and cash flow, and negotiating skills.
- Set up a program to minimize the commitment of funds to assets and fixed costs until you have revenues to justify them.
- Specified the characteristics of your target "first five" beneficiaries and set up a table to compare your expectations against the actual results, and are now analyzing and interpreting the differences for planning purposes.
- Put in place an operations program that is paying detailed attention to cash flow and quality.
- Continued testing assumptions at key checkpoints and redirected (and replanned) the project at any checkpoint where there is a significant difference between expected and actual.
- Revisited your Stakeholder Impact table to avoid getting blindsided by sociopolitical shifts.

Tough Love Test

If you answer no to any of the following questions, you might want to reconsider your venture strategy before moving ahead. If you answer no more than three times, you should seriously consider whether it is time to disengage. If you answer yes to all the following questions, you are ready to move on to the next chapter.

1. Do you have access to the selling, operating, cash flow management, and negotiating skills needed to manage the start-up?

2. Have you engineered a controlled launch rather than an up-front commitment of resources to a fixed course of action?
3. Have you planned to "earn the right to assets" rather than planned to purchase assets before you start?
4. Have you planned to "earn the right to fixed costs" rather than planned to pay out fixed costs ahead of revenues?
5. Do you have effective cash flow and quality monitoring and management procedures in place?
6. Have you instituted a "keeper of the assumptions" role and assigned it to someone whose task is to revisit the DDP and Stakeholder Impact table at each checkpoint, calling for a replanning session if necessary?

CHAPTER 13

Manage the Upside and Downside

Since social enterprises have a high probability of failure, the chances are pretty high that you will not be successful, and this means that a lot of attention needs to be given to the unpleasant but probable downside you could encounter. The problem is that, because of the uncertainty in which you operating, it may be hard to recognize that you are failing. In this chapter, we look at some of the things that will help prevent your continuing to pour resources and effort in the vain hope that "things may get better," a phenomenon Barry Staw called "escalation of commitment."[29]

We will cover the five things to do to manage the downside of your venture:

- Have a clear definition of failure at the start;
- Regularly monitor your sociopolitical situation;
- Preplan for disengagement should things go wrong;
- Monitor for the second-order (i.e., unintended) effects of your venture's success or failure; and
- Redirect your venture to where true opportunity lies, or launch a less sustainable enterprise that still accomplishes humanitarian good.

Define Failure

If you are not sure from the get-go what constitutes failure, there is every chance that, however well-intentioned, you will just keep going on and on with your venture—to no avail. Better to take the project off life support and redirect your energy and resources to some other project—heaven knows there are needs aplenty. Take care to articulate in your DDP, ahead of launch, what you regard as failure, using the framing from the planning phase to specify the minimum level of revenues and social impact delivered within a specified time, below which you will declare failure. For example, you may draw a line in the sand by saying, "If we are not making break-even cash flows and helping at least fifteen hundred people by January of such-and-such a year, we shall disengage."

Monitor the Sociopolitics

It is absolutely vital that as you launch your venture you keep a close eye on the stakeholders you identified in chapter 7. Use the tables from that chapter to carefully monitor the early responses from each stakeholder group, and consider the implications of responses that are different from those you predicted. It is imperative that you maintain a close watch on negative impacts and effectively deploy your strategies for dealing with them. In cases where you see major positive impacts, quickly communicate them to the respective stakeholders and use those impacts to validate their support of your venture. Confirmation of positive social impact is powerful ammunition as you try to mobilize inactive potential allies and needed indifferents to support you, and to dissuade or end-run inactive primary opponents.

In the Zambia Feeds case, the overwhelming success by small-scale growers gave Ilona sufficient support that she was able to successfully lobby the government's Department of Veterinary Livestock and Development to allow their veterinary assistants to participate in her educational seminars for new poultry growers by offering a technical services component (diseases, vaccines, and administration of drugs). Once given the opportunity to do so, the veterinary assistants not only proved to be willing and able to participate, but were important allies in improving poultry rearing practices and reducing the perceived risk of the activity in the eyes of naïve small-scale farmers.

In the AidsAid project, by using his connections with an Ivy medical school, and their connections with the government, Jaytee eventually secured a letter of authorization from a very senior official of the health department to develop the EMR system in the private clinic. This letter became an invaluable means to navigate the complex set of regulations in the country's health care industry and garner support for other necessary allies, such as the private clinic.

Preplan for Disengagement

While we are discussing unpleasant start-up preparation chores, let's look at the most psychologically difficult task, which is to *preplan* how you will disengage from the project in the event that it fails.

Here we are suggesting something nonintuitive and psycho-logically very challenging: Give careful thought as to how you intend to get *out* of the project before you even go in. This is tough—at this point in your venture you need to be gung-ho and ready to charge in, but at the same time you also have to be thinking about how to disengage!

Why? Since the probability of failing is high, the likelihood of the need to exit at some point is also high. The combination of high probability of exit and vulnerability of beneficiaries at exit suggests that social enterprises that anticipate exit will leave their beneficiaries better off than those that do not. As a custodian of scarce resources, it is prudent that you plan your exit before you even start, so that you do not create high dependency on the part of hapless beneficiaries and then leave them in the lurch because you do not have the funds to continue. The appropriate mind-set here is to plan to leave behind "a light footprint" in the event of your exit.

Let's review a few examples:

- **Zambia Feeds.** Although successful in meeting and exceeding societal and profitability objectives, Zambia Feeds has endured trials and tribulations along the way. Initially the targeted markets were small-scale farmers in rural areas. Although the target beneficiaries were willing participants, the logistical costs and market accessibility challenges made it impossible for would-be producers in more remote villages to raise and market chickens profitably. When the logistical vulnerability of remote village production became apparent in the more remote pilot villages, Ilona was able to redirect her efforts to villages closer to towns with adequate transportation infrastructure, long before the more remote pilots had built significant dependency on feed supplies.

- **AidsAid.** The pilot clinic was successful in delivering higher-quality patient care to a large number of HIV/AIDS patients and meeting the first phase of the project's social objectives. However, Jaytee was unable to identify and establish a viable revenue model, ultimately failing to meet his venture's commercial objectives. Throughout the venture, all stakeholders were kept informed as to progress, and all data were backed up and stored so that they would be transferable in the event of disengagement. During the venture, the existing patient management systems were kept running in parallel with the new EMR system. This served as a fallback: should the project fail, it would be possible to continue with the old, manual system at the clinic. It so happened that the preservation of the electronic data made it rather simple to transfer electronic records to the firm that took over from Jaytee, and the handover was pulled off with minimal disruption to clinic operations.

- **Khaya Cookie Company.** Polak's major attempt at scaling up commercial operations to the export markets was unsuccessful. However, the first business continues to operate in South Africa, supplying a number of hotels, retail stores, and an airline with hand-crafted, all-natural baked goods. This seed business has retained the majority of its original employees and trained many more, and has expanded operations. Polak is now managing a nonprofit in San Francisco that trains the unemployed in baking skills, and is again using piloting activities to deliver proof of concept before embarking on an ambitious expansion program.

- **Widows and Orphans Project.** This as yet unmentioned project was to train aging widows in small villages—caring for HIV/AIDS orphans —to rear chickens for an urban distributor. It is an example of a failure to prepare adequately for disengagement. The original project garnered a lot of attention by the public and senior politicians but ultimately failed to deliver the profits needed to keep it sustainable. Uncertainties in operations, transportation, working capital, and infrastructure proved to be large, expensive, and intractable impediments, as did recruiting a willing and capable entrepreneur. In spite of great demand from the many widows in the chosen region, the project proved to be commercially infeasible. Unfortunately, once the team had uncovered the magnitude of potential operations losses, the project—which had been started with the very best of intentions but with no preplanned disengagement—had to be terminated, and the women who had been signed up reverted to their former, very difficult circumstances. This resulted in significant negative publicity for the team, to whom blame for the disappointment was directed.

Monitor for Second-Order Effects

Second-order effects are (sometimes unintended) consequences of your venture's success. Based on our research, there are two types worth noting. First are positive effects of the progress of the venture, a "societal bonus" (as we shall see, second-order positive effects contribute to a venture's upside). Second are the negative effects this progress creates. These may be used by your opponents with inimical vested interests to justify their obstruction.

Let's review a few examples:

Zambia Feeds

Positive second-order effect: Because of the success of local chicken rearing, a number of other organizations, such as churches and prisons, have launched "out-grower" schemes, where they help set up poultry rearing activities and support the purchase of feeds and the sale of fowls by their constituents. These activities provide improved nutrition to their communities and also support the activities of Zambia Feeds through additional feed purchases.

Positive second-order effect: Because Zambia Feeds was able to sell increasing quantities of lower-cost, higher-quality feed in its region, competitors were eventually obliged to attempt to match Zambia Feeds' cost and quality, so that feed prices in real terms of all producers were lower in 2011 than in 2003, and at improved quality levels, thereby benefiting all poultry growers and reducing the cost of protein to consumers in the whole country, not just the immediate and underserved Zambia Feeds region.

Positive second-order effect: As a consequence of the success of Zambia Feeds, the poultry industry has expanded rapidly in the northwestern region, and in so doing, has spawned investment in poultry breeding facilities, distribution centers, and processing and packaging facilities, thereby creating economic opportunity for individuals as workers, raw material suppliers, and equipment service providers.

Negative second-order effect: Feathers are the only part of a chicken that the local people do not eat. The proliferation of small chicken farms in the region has led to a problem with chicken feathers, which the less responsible farmers simply discard after the bird has been plucked, leaving unsightly accumulations of feathers around the villages. Still, with the right type of combustion, it is possible to burn the feathers without generating noxious fumes. There is a project under way to investigate how to burn feathers, thus recovering energy and at the same time solving the problem of accumulating feathers.

Negative second-order effect: Some farmers use chicken compost to fertilize their nearby vegetable patches. The proximity of the vegetables patches to the chicken rearing area represents a biosecurity hazard to the new batches of chicks and increases the presence of flies. This compost can be removed from the site by selling it to vegetable farmers who do not raise poultry, or by disposing of it in pits and sprinkling it with lime.

AidsAid

Positive second-order effect: Large-scale success would extend the lifespan and vitality of HIV/AIDS patients, whose period of labor output could be lengthened with resulting economic benefit for the economy in a country whose population is being hollowed out by AIDS-related illnesses.

Potential negative second-order effect: There was a danger that wide-scale increases in vitality would lead HIV/AIDS to be ingenuously viewed as "manageable" and therefore not feared as much as a "terminal" disease, causing a reduction in preventive practices.

Khaya Cookie Company

Positive second-order effect: Younger employees have moved on to attend trade schools and even college, and/or have found employment, due to increased employability, in other businesses.

Potential negative second-order effect: As the employed women earned income and saved money, they ran the risk of becoming targets of theft and "sources of borrowing" from husbands, family members, and people in their community. This concern echoes recent examples of such negative second-order effects in the microfinance industry of India, where family members have pressured eligible women to increase borrowing to unsustainable levels of debt.

What should you do about negative second-order effects? The problem is that they are not necessarily obvious. We suggest you make it a habit of brainstorming with your advisors on this, doing two types of exercise:

1. Create a simple "impact map," depicting your answers to the questions:
    -   If our venture is successful, what other factors will be positively or negatively affected?
    -   If that happens, what other factors will be positively or negatively affected?

Then discuss what indicators would signal that these second-order effects were starting to kick in, and monitor those indicators.

2. Revisit the Beneficiary Experience and Deliverables tables from chapters 4, 5, and 6 and, for each step, ask:
    -   What might the consequences be of major success at this step?
    -   What would the positive and/or negative second-order effects be of significantly increasing activity at this step?

Then set up indicators and monitor them.

An example from Zambia Feeds was the realization that significant growth in the rearing of chickens in the region might begin to strain the supply of baby chicks, particularly at times of the year when demand for poultry increased, such as at Christmas.

Ilona worked with chick suppliers to put in place a system of booking orders for chicks ahead of peak demand periods. Although not 100% successful, the system, and Ilona's pre-booked orders, persuaded chick suppliers to expand their capacity by investing in new production facilities ahead of current demand.

Redirect Your Project, or Launch a Different Enterprise Entirely

While we are passionate about creating a profit-generating entity that attacks a social problem, we are not obsessed with doing so. This brings us to a very important point for organizations or individuals who are *not* looking for an *entrepreneurship* approach to a social problem. We believe that:

- Even if you are not intent on a profitable solution, starting off by trying to find a profitable way of attacking a problem *forces* people to be very parsimonious with resources in their operations.
- If you cannot find a way to be profitable, just thinking about how to establish your venture profitably will almost always lead to more efficient funding allocations at its launch.

If you can't make a profit, there are decreasingly sustainable but nonetheless plausible alternative approaches, which we call redirection down an *aspirations cascade*. Let's look at these as possible alternatives to giving up entirely.

Migrating Down the Aspirations Cascade

If, during the course of your controlled launch, you learn that your project will not be profitable, you don't necessarily have to walk away. There may be an opportunity to reduce your profit aspiration levels *and* still continue to impact beneficiaries positively.

With an aspirations cascade, we consider social impact per dollar (or relevant currency) consumed over time and then broadly categorize ventures based on the degree to which they require funding for operations and asset replacement. (For a discussion of operating costs and asset replacement, see chapter 9.)

It may be necessary to migrate your enterprise down the aspirations cascade. The five enterprises that make up the aspirations cascade, from top to bottom, are market-scalers, self-sustainers, break-even operators, partial leveragers, and reliants.

Market-scaler. At the top (and most desired level) of our aspirations cascade we have the enterprise that we hope will meet *our* avowed aspiration: to generate sustainable and growing profits, subject *primarily* to the delivery of an attractive minimum social impact. A market-scaler is a successful social enterprise that has the ability to significantly scale up growth on both the social benefit and profit dimensions, and in so doing, to attract resources for growth from the market at large. This enterprise generates the highest level of social impact per dollar expended over time. A distinctive feature of this type of enterprise, relative to those that come below it on the aspirations cascade, is its ability to raise capital from private-sector institutions such as banks and for-profit corporations, which typically do not invest in nonprofits. (Conversely, many nonprofit funding organizations are unable or unwilling to fund for-profit activities.) Once a venture is self-sustaining, it no longer draws from the lean resources available for the social sector. If, in fact, a profitable venture is created, not only do the immediate beneficiaries receive benefits, but the venture begins to pay taxes, further contributing to society. In the case of Zambia Feeds, as part of its corporate social responsibility program, the parent company began supporting several nonprofit programs such as jails and church groups, whose prisoners and impoverished parishioners, respectively, became involved in farming chickens for consumption.

Self-sustainer. If the social enterprise cannot deliver growth-generating profits, the project can be migrated down one level on the aspirations cascade to become a fully self-sustaining nonprofit that generates enough net revenues to cover all operating costs and replace depreciated (used-up) assets. This is an appealing proposition to the types of donors and philanthropists who are attracted by the opportunity to seed/establish an organization that attends to a worthy cause and is thereafter able to continue to do so without the need for repeat funding.

Break-even operator. If full self-sufficiency is not possible or appropriate, the project migrates down a level to a nonprofit that covers all its operating costs but needs periodic funding infusions to pay for assets and asset replacement.

Partial leverager. This venture, which includes NGOs/nonprofits, requires periodic funding but generates some net revenue from its operations.

Reliant. Once all alternatives are exhausted, you might migrate your project down the cascade into a pure-play charity. Charities are not second-class citizens! There are many noble and deserving charities attending to desperate needs. Using the tools in this book, they may be able to do even more good with their limited resources. The discipline of forcing even nonprofits and charities to think hard about making a profit or generating revenues reduces the cost of whatever format is finally selected.

Figure 13.1 illustrates the cascade from the highest level of social impact per dollar outcome (market-scaler) through organizations (charities) that are fully reliant on donations.

Figure 13.1: Aspirations Cascade: Moderating Income Ambitions

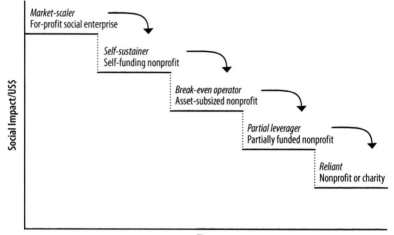

Figure 13.2: Aspirations Cascade: Amplifying Social Impact

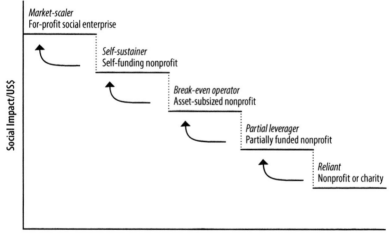

If you are unable to meet one of or both your objectives (i.e., profit and social impact), you may begin to consider changing your enterprise's current format. This can be done by migrating down the aspirations cascade (perhaps moving down the cascade more than one level). In essence, you disengage from your original organizational format and reengage within the same environment but using another organizational format. For example, in the AidsAid case, it became clear, after multiple redirections and the impacts of the 2008 financial crisis, that the entrepreneurial team was unable to create a new and sustainable revenue model. But because a large number of patients were benefitting from the program, the team elected to transfer the operation and patient data to a fully funded nonprofit entity. Thus, AidsAid moved from being a social enterprise with market-scaler aspirations on the aspirations cascade to a partial leverager. Once all data had been transferred to the nonprofit, the project was handed over with minimal inconvenience to any of the beneficiaries or to the clinic.

If your organization happens to be at the lower levels of the Aspirations Cascade, you may want to seek ways to generate revenues and thereby increase your social impact, as show in Figure 13.2. Managers can therefore be encouraged to consider how to move to the next level up the cascade. This frees up resources and funding to introduce new beneficiaries into their program.

In addition, a charity could focus on enhancing the lives of some of the beneficiaries enough so that a percentage of them would become self-sufficient. These beneficiaries would thus be able to migrate upstream. If nonprofits and charities make it a practice to build self-sufficiency for some of their beneficiaries, those beneficiaries can gradually go from being recipients of charity to being self-sufficient, thereby making space in the charity for new beneficiaries.

This is not a pipe dream, and it is exactly what one of our current projects is exploring. Communities in Malawi are looking to use the profits from a volunteer community farming enterprise to pay for the schooling of AIDS orphans, who can use the education they get to seek employment. The project's founders expect that some of the educated orphans will one day be able to manage the farming activity and expand it to new villages.

Note that earlier we suggested you clearly define failure—remember that if you reach your definition, it is time to disengage. Should you reach the point where you are unable to meet your social impact and profit objectives, and if you are unable to migrate down the aspirations cascade, it is time to implement your preplanned disengagement.

We have observed a number of social entrepreneurs reach this point, and for those who did not clearly define failure a *priori*, it was a traumatic and debilitating experience. Given the deep empathy inherent in social entrepreneurs, it is sometimes more difficult, and takes longer, for them to disengage from a project—and therefore failure of such projects end up being more expensive. Social enterprises must guard vigilantly against escalation of commitment. Once commitment escalates, it becomes all the more difficult for social enterprises to cut their losses and disengage from the situation. Social considerations and guilt associated with leaving beneficiaries without a suitable alternative can further impede disengagement. Self-discipline is therefore critical to effectively managing the process and your stakeholders.

If you are doing what we recommended in this chapter, you can forge ahead. Good luck to you and good fortune to your beneficiaries!

Chapter Checklist

After working through the processes outlined in this chapter, you will be doing or will have done the following:

- ○ Put together a definition of failure and a disengagement plan.
- ○ Celebrated early, even if modest, successes and recognized those on your team responsible for them.

○ Spent time with your advisory group working through your revised Beneficiary Experience and Deliverables tables to identify and put in place any warning signals of both negative and positive second-order effects.

○ Recognized that aspirations cascades represent options for changes in mission or strategy from one enterprise type to another, and (for projects under profit duress) looked at alternative organizational formats in the cascade.

Tough Love Test

If you answer no to any of the following questions, you might want to reconsider your venture strategy before moving ahead. If you answer no three times or more, you should seriously consider whether it is time to disengage. If you answer yes to all the following questions, by all means, begin to gear up for scale-up.

1. Have you put together a definition of failure that your advisors approve of? Have you preplanned disengagement?

2. Are you confident that your enterprise is sociopolitically safe and suitably insulated from interference?

3. Have you brainstormed possible second-order effects from the success of your enterprise, and put in place a set of early-warning signals for these effects?

4. If you do not appear to have a market-scaler venture, have you considered which enterprise lower down on the aspirations cascade yours might be, and at what point you might migrate there?

CHAPTER 14

Scale Up Your Social Enterprise

Once you have your pilot behind you, and you have established a sound start-up operation, the next big step is to decide if you want to extend the scope of your social impact. If you decide to grow your social enterprise, the key strategic decision is *how* you intend to scale it up. You have two different modalities to choose from:

- **Cookie-cutter.** This strategy involves replicating existing operations in other geographic locations.
- **Expansion from the core.** This strategy involves expanding operations at a single site in order to support the growing demand for the enterprise's product or services.

As you consider your business model, your beneficiaries, and available resources, determine the most appropriate method of scaling up. In some instances, you may decide to use a sequential combination of both strategies, but you should generally select just one to start. Each of the scale-up strategies has nuances to which you must attend. For example, a cookie-cutter strategy will usually require a higher number of middle managers, due to the dispersed nature of activities. It will also mean not being able to capture economies of scale. Furthermore, you will need to deal with the logistical challenge of operating manifold supply chains to and from each location.

An expansion from the core at a single site may represent simpler management and logistics challenges due to the concentration of operations in one location. However, in the event of a system failure, the core is exposed to massive downside—versus the cookie-cutter strategy, which allows you to keep going with the other "cookies" if one cookie fails.

As you begin to think about how to scale up, use your newly developed skills to create a DDP for whatever modality, or modality combination, you choose. Though the uncertainty will have been reduced, it is still better to use a DDP and to identify, once again, your key assumptions and your vulnerability if those assumptions end up being wrong.

No matter which mode of scale-up you select, there will be challenges. When you start your social enterprise, you typically deal with a few intractable problems in your initial transactions. However, as you begin to scale up, the nature and number of problems shift— from a few critical challenges to more and more problems caused by the scale-up itself and the increased activities of a larger operation. The problems typically become smaller in scope and more tractable, but they also become more and more frequent and pressing. So the real danger is that, if you're not careful, you end up being distracted by problem overload, which results in a loss of focus on the most important drivers of success.

In this chapter, we lay out the five key challenges you are likely to face, regardless of which mode of scale-up you choose:

- Hazards of visibility
- Strains on your ecosystem
- Internal resource pressures
- Management challenges
- Anticipating bigness

Given your choice of scale-up strategy, think carefully about how to deal with each of these generic scale-up challenges.

Table 14.1 provides an overview of the shift in problem structure as you move from start-up to scale-up. Note the left-hand column, "From," in which there are relatively few, seemingly intractable problems; and the right-hand column, "To," in which there are many, smaller but more frequent, and more pressing, problems.

Table 14.1: Scale-Up Challenges

From few, seemingly intractable problems	To many, smaller, pressing problems
1. Hazards of visibility	
a) No or little competition	Increasingly aggressive competition
b) Minor attention from authorities	Increasing interventions by authorities
c) Tolerance from vested interests	Significant attention and perhaps obstruction from vested interests
d) Grateful labor force	Emergence of "organized" labor force
2. Strains on your ecosystem	
a) Supply creation—finding reliable sources of quality supply	Suppliers' system overloading—reductions in reliability and quality, increased supplier pricing demands
b) Convincing distributors to sign up	Distributors rationing limited supplies to "favorites"; gouging prices
c) Beneficiaries content to wait (when they can)	Escalating beneficiary demands/expectations
d) Employees grateful for work opportunity	Trained employees moving to alternative opportunities you have "up-skilled" them to pursue
3. Internal resource pressures	
a) Marketing trying to generate few, early sales	Marketing identifying and serving growing numbers of segments
b) Production trying to deliver adequate low-volume quality	Production maintaining reliability of output, quality, and equipment upkeep under capacity overload
c) Finance seeking limited start-up funds	Finance scrambling to fund growing liquid assets and then capacity expansion
d) Your personally securing small qualified workforce	Human resources recruiting, training, and motivating growing workforce

Note: Table 14.1 continues on following page.

Table 14.1: Scale-Up Challenges *(Continued)*

From few, seemingly intractable problems	To many, smaller, pressing problems
4. Management challenges	
a) Management by direct supervision	Recruitment of uncompromisingly qualified middle managers. Induction via task force teams to assimilate newcomers
b) Management of small, "connected" workforce	Management directed through supervisors (with feelings of abandonment by early employees)
c) Management values conveyed "one on one"	Management values conveyed through orientation programs and demonstration of values
d) Managing everything yourself	Decisions to be made on tasks to be delegated, to whom, and when
5. Anticipating bigness	
a) No need for functional experts	Need to build professional finance/accounting and human resources departments
b) Recruiting and training as needed	Recruiting and training ahead of needs
c) Raising funds as needed	Planning ahead for major project and enterprise financing

We shall discuss each problem and showcase examples to illustrate them. Forgive us for drawing liberally from our experience with Zambia Feeds, since it has been the longest-running and most successful of the social enterprises created in the Social Entrepreneurship Program. It has scaled up to a significant enterprise—with all the attendant scale-up problems.

Hazards of Visibility

The price of success is visibility, an often-overlooked aspect of becoming a larger organization. Visibility can frequently be positive, as it garners support for the social enterprise, but it can also raise challenges for you and your team in the form of competitive response, unexpected behavior by authorities, changes in the behavior of vested interest groups, and worker disruption through organizing efforts. Let's review each in a little more detail.

Shift from No or Little Competition to Increasingly Aggressive Competition

First and foremost, success attracts competition. Initially you pose little threat to anybody. But as you start to grow, you attract the attention of any existing competitors who initially didn't care too much about you. Alternatively, your success is likely to precipitate new competition. Perversely, in the social enterprise world, pre-cipitating competition can actually be a positive outcome for the beneficiaries: more people get helped as the scale of competition increases. This, of course, does not absolve you from the need to generate enough profits and profitability for your own social impact to have sustained growth.

Zambia Feeds. Once the young Zambia Feeds business was gener-ating meaningful feed sales, Ilona received information that her rapid growth had attracted the attention of the larger, established competitors in the major urban parts of Zambia. The "word on the street" was that the competition was considering a significant across-the-board price cut in an attempt to force Zambia Feeds out of business. In June of 2003, Ilona aggressively engaged with partners and consultants to identify cost-reduction possibilities with which to improve Zambia Feeds' ability to compete during a protracted price war, should one develop. Her efforts were successful, and she managed to deploy linear programming and operations scheduling to sufficiently reduce her production costs and selling prices while maintaining high quality. Her venture continued to operate—in fact, to thrive—with a much lower cost structure.

Shift from Minor Attention from Authorities to Increasing Interventions by Authorities

While you are small, you may not attract much attention from ranking members of the community or government. However, once your enterprise begins to look attractive or begins to disrupt existing social structures or payment streams, you are likely to experience significant changes in attitude toward your activities. This can raise two problems among local authorities: First, they notice you and can begin to invoke or generate regulations that increase your costs. Second, in some situations, they will now see this as an opportunity to extract income or revenues from you by withholding permits unless you do something to "help" them.

Fish farming operation. "No, it must be mobile," said the prospective entrepreneur, looking away. We were standing in a field with a would-be fish farmer in Africa a few years ago, and he was refusing an offer to pilot a small fish farming operation. We had been asked by a local entrepreneur, our host, to help design a fish production system that would produce relatively low-cost protein and create many small-scale production opportunities for interested entrepreneurs in the area. Somewhat perplexed, our host asked why a less efficient mobile option, rather than the system we were proposing—a much more reliable production system already designed to be built as concrete ponds embedded in the ground—was a must-have. The prospective entrepreneur looked at us and said, "If I do all the work to start the farm, and I succeed, then the chief decides that he wants the fish farm now that it is up and running, and he will simply take it over. If it is a mobile system, I can dismantle the plant and put it up elsewhere." And with that, the entire project needed to be reconfigured.

A critical lesson we learned is that you need to approach and reach an agreement with influential stakeholders *before* you commence scale-up. The terms of the agreement should be clearly spelled out and agreed upon by the most senior members of the local authorities. Where possible, national-level agreements might need to be put in place, so as to provide some measure of defense against unanticipated interference at the local level.

Shift from Tolerance from Vested Interests to Significant Attention and Perhaps Obstruction from Vested Interests

As we have said, often parties have vested interests in the perpetuation of the problem, or continuation of the status quo. In the beginning, they may leave you alone and simply regard you as a minor (and more than likely, temporary) nuisance. But as you begin to have greater impact on the system to which they are accustomed, they may actively obstruct you or set in motion processes to make your life more difficult.

Khaya Cookie Company. As Polak's cookie business started to grow, the community leaders became aware of the increasing commercial activity around the formerly unused facility she had leased from them, and they saw the opportunity to extract more rent for the facility. They asked for considerably more money (which, in effect, would have caused the enterprise's insolvency), threatening to withdraw permission for baking operations if it were not paid.

Shift from a Grateful Labor Force to the Emergence of Organized Labor

In the beginning, your labor force may be happy just to have a job, but as you start to grow, you need to anticipate that the workforce may not remain perfectly happy. Indeed, some workers may begin to organize, perhaps informally, and make demands on you because they feel that since you are doing well, they should do better than they are. What might happen is that, for the first time, you will be observed and targeted by formal labor organizations that see an opportunity to expand their membership base by securing your labor force. Unionization of your workforce, or even informal organization of your workers, with its attendant increases in costs and organizational complexity, is something you may need to anticipate and prepare to manage as efficiently and effectively as possible.

Zambia Feeds. Organized labor unions spent a number of years mobilizing a core group of Zambia Feeds employees, who ultimately succeeded in motivating sufficient numbers of their coworkers to join the union, thereafter obliging management to recognize and negotiate with the union as legitimate representation of the workers' interests.

Strains on Your Ecosystem

Shift from Supplier Creation to Suppliers' System Overloading

At the onset of your social enterprise, you may find it necessary to create a supply chain for yourself (perhaps such suppliers did not exist before) by convincing people and businesses who can make what you need, of the quality you need, when you need it. This may require that you bring in resources from outside the geographic area in which your venture is located.

As your venture expands, and your demands on your various suppliers grow, you might begin to exceed the capacity of the supply system in place. This is likely to have negative effects on both your enterprise and your beneficiaries. For example, an overloaded supplier may begin to deliver subpar-quality supplies or services. Furthermore, there may come a point where suppliers recognize they have supplier power and begin to raise their prices, all of which impacts your reputation, profits, and profitability.

Be on the lookout for emerging evidence of supplier overload and supplier power behavior. Give thought to managing your suppliers in accordance with your own demands—training and assisting them if necessary—so that they continue to support you and your objectives.

Zambia Feeds. In the early days of rapid growth, Zambia Feeds' customers were unable to secure sufficient supplies of chicks during peak demand periods preceding national holidays. As a consequence, Zambia Feeds' own sales were adversely affected, and inventory levels rose rapidly. The following season and thereafter, Zambia Feeds worked with chick suppliers to forecast seasonal demands more accurately and to prepare suppliers for the sometimes large fluctuations in orders.

Shift from Convincing Distributors to Sign Up to Distributors Rationing Limited Supplies and Gouging Prices

As a *de novo* start-up, with no track record and little credibility, you may have to go out and beg people to distribute for you. In the case of Zambia Feeds, distributors had to be convinced and, in some cases, created—by persuading local trading stores to stock feed on consignment. As you begin to grow, and the demand for your product grows, you might begin to run out of capacity to supply sufficient quantities to meet your distributors' orders. In this case, there is a danger that distributors will respond to your inability to meet their demands by repricing their limited deliveries as they see fit, and rationing—that is, choosing which beneficiaries are served and which are not, and at what prices. A sure way to create irate customers is to have a distributor serve the needs of one large customer at the expense of many smaller ones. You need to plan who will do the rationing: Do *you* decide which customers will get your limited supplies, or do you allow distributors to supply their favorites or gouge customers with higher prices?

Zambia Feeds. Production breakdowns periodically affected delivery to distributors. During such times, Ilona was fast to respond and engage with her distributors. She and her sales team negotiated which customers received supplies and when. Available supplies were allocated fairly across Zambia Feeds' portfolio of customers. In this way, customers were warned of impending shortfalls in supply so they could adjust their chick purchasing and raising schedules, and not find themselves with a coop full of starving birds.

Shift from Beneficiaries Content to Wait to Beneficiaries with Escalating Demands and Expectations

In the early days of your enterprise, it will not be unusual for your beneficiaries to be happy just to have your product or service. You must ensure that you are able to deliver what your beneficiaries have ordered and maintain quality while doing so. For example, do you have sufficient and reliable transportation? Are you able to finance sufficient finished goods and raw materials inventories?

As demand starts to grow, beneficiaries become used to experiencing your offering and its benefits and will become annoyed and angry should there be an interruption in timely service. Their level of patience will gradually decline as their expectations for your products or services rise. One of your primary objectives is to assist beneficiaries in attaining a higher standard of living. In many cases, this will involve helping them develop an income stream upon which they will become dependent. You should expect that any threat to that income stream will be met with a high degree of frustration and may provoke angry reaction.

It is often cheaper to buy by forward contract and be secure in the knowledge that you will be able to deliver to your beneficiary expectations rather than fall short and risk losing these customers to emergent competitors. However, this capability requires access to capital at an acceptable cost in order to finance the inventory.

Zambia Feeds. Zambia Feeds must commit to a certain tonnage of soybeans before the crop is harvested so as to ensure it has sufficient soybean cake inventory for production. Soybeans are harvested once a year and are often in short supply and priced high between seasons.

Shift from Employees Grateful for Work to Trained Employees Moving to Alternative Opportunities

Initially your employees might be perfectly happy just to have a job, as it is an opportunity to generate income for them and their families. Your training them to do the job is an investment for you. To their advantage (and to your credit), they become increasingly employable, not just within your enterprise but also elsewhere, using the very skills you helped them develop. This is good from a social perspective, as the more people out there with needed skills, the better for the economy and society. However, you will then have the added burden of replacing such workers after having invested in their training. In some cases, emergent competitors will recognize the quality of your training-and-development program and actively target your employees as prospective candidates for their own firms, thereby making you a source of skills development and labor supply, and increasing your operations costs.

AidsAid. The AidsAid project frequently suffered the loss of key programming talent. This is a particularly poignant example of the ability of skilled workers in near-Knightian environments to move frequently for higher pay elsewhere. Not only did management have to attend to the disruption caused by the immediate loss of programmers who resigned, but it also had to lay out significantly higher programming costs than budgeted, to pay for the emergency services of skilled programmers flown in from elsewhere on temporary work permits.

Internal Resource Pressures

As your enterprise starts to grow, so will internal pressures. In general, when scaling up, you move from a position in which one manager runs everything to a position where one manager is no longer sufficient. As a result, you will need to build several types of functional capability, function by function.

Shift from Marketing Trying to Generate a Few Early Sales to Marketing Identifying and Serving a Growing Number of Segments

Initially you are concerned with getting the first few sales in the book and delivered. But as you start to scale up, the primary job of marketing becomes identifying, targeting, and servicing the most important segments of beneficiaries. Segmentation begins to take on a much more important role as you decide which of the growing segments your operation can best serve, bearing in its mind that your mission is to balance helping targeted beneficiaries with generating financial results sufficient to sustain your enterprise. You are forced to move from self-marketing to a more formal organizational marketing process. It is therefore incumbent upon you to give sufficient thought to how your marketing capability is going to be developed and delivered ahead of need.

Zambia Feeds. Zambia Feeds developed a sales force and marketing team over time, both of which worked together to build customer management systems based on marketing analytics such as geographic location, frequency of purchase, size of purchase, and local influence of beneficiaries. When Zambia Feeds started, it had no competitors in its region within its chosen customer segments. Once the enterprise had grown in stature and expanded geographically, its current and prospective customers expected it to operate wherever its competitors were operational. For example, customers, industry authorities, and even competitors expected Zambia Feeds to participate in the annual national and regional agricultural shows. While Zambia Feeds could use these shows to highlight its products and services, this meant that core marketing and sales personnel had to attend each show, and were therefore not with their customers in their respective sales regions during the events.

Shift from Production Delivering Adequate Low-Volume Quality to Production Maintaining Reliability of Output, Equipment Upkeep, and Quality under Capacity Overload

You started by attempting to deliver adequate amounts of product at relatively low volumes (you were just getting started), at adequate levels of quality. As you begin to grow, the challenge becomes how to sustain reliable output. With increasing volumes, you need to sustain scheduling and quality management under increasing production pressures. You will also need to ensure that your equipment is suitably maintained, and that you have enough capacity. This becomes particularly difficult when following a cookie-cutter strategy, because you have to manage these issues in many places, and you can physically be in only one place at a time. It is therefore essential to begin thinking how to create sufficient management capacity to execute your intended strategy. This means that before you scale up, you may have to train management ahead of needing them.

Zambia Feeds. As Zambia Feeds began to experience increasing demands on its production capacity, under pressure to produce ever-increasing targets, employees occasionally mixed large batches of feed inconsistently and therefore delivered lower-quality product to the market. It is mission-critical that animal feed consistency be maintained in order for beneficiaries to raise poultry reliably. Incorrectly formulated feed has the potential to kill young chicks, thereby immediately compromising the farmer. Ilona was forced to begin automating production with industrial-grade mixers, in order to maintain reliability at higher levels of production. These expenses will be further addressed under financing issues.

Shift from Finance Seeking Limited Start-Up Funds to Finance Scrambling to Fund Growing Liquid Assets and Capacity Expansion

When you started out, you sought out a limited number of start-up funds. Now, as you grow, particularly under rapid scale-up, you see a dramatic increase in the need for liquid assets (i.e., inventory and receivables), which puts the enterprise under cash flow pressure. What you need now are people who understand cash flow management and the basic principles of financing a growing operation.

AidsAid. A lower-level bookkeeper was unaware of a change in the national tax code. This change in tax assessment represented a massive potential future tax obligation, which was both unanticipated and unknown prior to a formal inquiry by the tax department. This expense was large enough to threaten the solvency of the clinic, and the clinic owner spent a significant amount of time trying to raise funds to meet the obligation and hire tax advisors to negotiate on her behalf. Had there been in place a suitably qualified accountant, the entire episode may have been prevented.

Shift from Your Personally Securing a Small, Qualified Workforce to Human Resources Recruiting, Training, and Motivating a Growing Workforce

At the launch of your enterprise you may have identified and recruited a small labor force; perhaps you even had to train a number of them. As you start to scale up, however, your need for people will grow, which means you will need more sophisticated ways of recruiting, training, and motivating this growing workforce. Perhaps the most important role you have in managing scale-up is to recruit and train the very best workers available, and letting go those who don't work out—both of which require discipline and steadfastness. It is your responsibility to determine the performance standards of each employee function and to ensure that none be allowed to jeopardize the expectations and standards you set. The last thing you want is to employ inadequately skilled staff and subsequently witness your organization falter and your time become increasingly diverted from the organization's mission.

Management Challenges

Shift from Management by Direct Supervision to Recruitment of Uncompromisingly Qualified Middle Managers

In the beginning the management of your organization was executed by you, and you provided direct supervision and control over the activities of everyone in the firm. As your venture grows, however, particularly with a cookie-cutter strategy, you will need middle managers. In uncertain environments, middle managers are usually scarce, if available at all. Thus, you will need a process to select and train middle management and develop their ability to execute in your absence without needing to turn to you to solve small daily problems. In other words, you need to think about those functions you will delegate, to whom, when, and where. When discussing organizational scale-up, one of our favorite serial entrepreneurs likes to use the phrase "If you fail to develop effective middle management in time, you become like a spider trapped in its own web."

Zambia Feeds. Ilona faced constant challenges in developing the skill sets of middle managers operating distribution centers. Given its relatively short shelf life, it is critical that feed be rotated correctly through the distribution facility using the first in, first out method. Inventory that is held longer than its useful shelf life will spoil and must then be thrown away.

Shift from Management of Small, "Connected" Workforce to Management through Supervisors

During the start-up phase, the team is small, and everyone is connected to you and to one another. With scale-up and the move to management through supervisors, you lose the personal touch with employees that you had in the beginning. Now someone else is directing employees' activities within the enterprise, which can lead to feelings of abandonment by them: "He does not care about us anymore." "She never speaks to us." We have observed this multiple times in the field, the consequence being a gradual demotivation of employees who value the intimacy of a small firm. You must develop an internal strategy to wean employees off direct interaction with you and onto your emerging middle management team.

Shift from Management Values Conveyed "One on One" to Management Values Conveyed through Orientation Programs and Demonstration of Values

You initially brought a set of values to your enterprise that were conveyed one on one by the decisions you made and the discussions you had with the people who reported to you. As your venture grows, and particularly with dispersed management, the sets of values somehow need to be transferred to employees in other, sometimes remote locations. This may have to be done through the use of orientation programs in which the values of the company, the basic rules of conduct, and the expectations for each employee are clearly articulated. This requires forethought with respect to the appropriate messages and communication channels. It also takes time. Consider developing a powerful induction program that both you and your most senior managers attend. This is not something you can delegate during the early stages of scale-up, because if you show that you are too busy to pay attention to the values you espouse, no one else will pay attention to them, either.

Zambia Feeds. Ilona developed a simple but effective method of induction for new operations workers. New workers were taken on as temporary hires until they had proven themselves within the organization. During their induction phase, they were required to wear a different color overall from those of the full-time workers, who monitored and managed these new hires. The middle management team assessed each temporary worker and was involved in deciding whether to hire them full time.

Shift from Managing Everything Yourself to Deciding Which Tasks Will Be Delegated, to Whom, and When

This self-evident need often goes unattended (despite its self-evidence), as owners allow themselves to be trapped in their own webs. It is crucial that you remain aware of your personal time constraints during scale-up. A good way of doing so is simply to look at your calendar and the number of hours per day available to you during the start-up phase. Then continue to do so as the demands on your time increase with the size of your organization. While your obligations to organization management increase dramatically, your hours available per day do not. It is vital, therefore, to plan ahead, and decide which tasks will be delegated, to whom, and when. As you do so, remember that members of your management team need to be trained to take on their new roles without disruption to you or the organization.

Anticipating Bigness

Shift from No Need for Functional Experts to Need to Build Finance/Accounting and Human Resources Departments

In the beginning you may not need functional experts, as you are running the enterprise yourself. For example, you may be doing your own production scheduling, marketing strategies, management accounting, and operations oversight. However, as your venture grows, you will need departments that perform these tasks. You cannot spend your time keeping the books yourself. You will also need a legitimate human resources department to think aggressively about recruiting, training, staffing, and promotion systems. This is mission-critical as you develop a stable and competitive larger enterprise.

During this process, it is paramount that you think through the more important areas versus the less important, as you will need to delegate when you are no longer able to manage everything yourself.

Zambia Feeds. As Zambia Feeds expanded, Ilona first hired a manager to head up the administration function. This role was expanded to include a small human resources department, the responsibility of which was to manage and develop the growing workforce and to serve as the primary liaison between workers, management, and a labor union once one was formally represented within the enterprise. The manager later reported to a chief financial officer, who was in turn responsible for all group finance and accounting.

Shift from Recruiting and Training as Needed to Recruiting and Training Ahead of Needs

During the enterprise launch, you recruited and trained as needed. With scale-up, the number of people you need to recruit expands dramatically, thus requiring a formal system to recruit people ahead of when you need them and not after you need them—usually when it is too late. Remember that in many high-uncertainty environments there is seldom a ready supply of the skills and capabilities required for effective management of a growing enterprise.

AidsAid. Jaytee sent the AidsAid project manager to short courses in the United States to learn the basic requirements of an effective EMR system. Once she had been trained, she was in a position to develop local skills in accurate EMR creation and main-tenance.

This training made her eminently more employable in her area (and at risk of going elsewhere—a problem we have already discussed).

Shift from Raising Funds as Needed to Planning Ahead for Major Enterprise Financing

When you launched your venture, you calculated the required funds for proof-of-concept and planned to learn rapidly at low cost, all the while allowing for redirection as you learned. Now, as you consider strategic scale-up requirements, you may need more sophisticated financial planning capabilities. In other words, you may need to convince banks or investors *ahead of time* of the value and attractiveness of capital expansion plans, using well-developed project and enterprise assessment techniques.

Now refer back to your Funding table (chapter 6) to review funding needs and potential sources of funds. In particular, consider capital expense needs: What assets do you require to facilitate your scale-up needs? Are they available on lease, at acceptable terms? If not, can you get them used? If not, what options are available for the purchase of new equipment?

Once you have determined what assets are necessary, you can begin to consider the funding sources currently available. Remember, once you begin to purchase assets— particularly expensive assets upon which you pay interest for borrowed funds—you have effectively increased your fixed overhead costs. If you borrow funds from a bank, for example, you will be required to pay interest on the principal, as well as eventually repay the loan.

Chapter Checklist

Following the processes in this chapter, you will have:

- ○ Determined the most appropriate growth strategy for your social enterprise, namely a cookie-cutter strategy or an expansion from the core (or a combination of the two).

○ Considered the hazards of visibility and prepared your social enterprise to defend against or attend to each hazard as it emerges.

○ Planned to develop your supplier and distribution systems ahead of growth, in order to mitigate the organizational strains brought on by that growth.

○ Carefully considered the implications of key employee attrition, developed a compensation strategy to keep those employees most important to you, and prepared a replacement plan for those who leave.

○ Developed an explicit "middle management to development" plan, which includes a plan for work prioritization and delegation.

○ Developed an internal strategy to wean employees off direct interaction with you and onto your emerging middle management team.

○ Planned to build administrative functional departments, such as finance/accounting and human resources, to provide a stable internal platform for enterprise scale-up.

○ Carefully considered the financial implications of your scale-up strategy and identified the available and appropriate sources of major financing.

Tough Love Test

If you answer no to any of the following questions, you have work to do, and you might want to reconsider your timetable or path to scale. If you answer no more than three times, you are not ready for scale-up. If you answer yes to all the following questions, you are ready to proceed with your plan to scale up your social enterprise. Good luck!

1. Have you identified the key hazards to your social enterprise as it begins to scale up and becomes more visible? Do you have a plan to mitigate or preemptively deal with such challenges?

2. Are you confident that your supplier base has the capacity to support your growth while maintaining quality and reliability of supply?

3. Are you confident that your distribution system has the capacity to support your growth without compromising delivery reliability and your customer base?

4. Have you identified appropriate middle management team members to whom you will delegate key administrative responsibility (e.g., marketing and sales, production management, finance and administration, and HR recruitment and training)?

5. Are you convinced that the skills required to support an effective scale-up strategy exist and are accessible to you? If not, have you developed a plausible plan to develop high-potential employees within an acceptable time frame and at an acceptable cost?

6. Have you calculated the resources required to support your scale-up? Are you confident in your ability to secure those resources?

Conclusion

If you have survived all the Tough Love Tests we've posed, you should be well on your way to operating a growing and profit-generating enterprise that is delivering increasing social benefits to an increasing number of beneficiaries and is poised to scale up. That, of course, is the purpose of this book, and we are thrilled that you have come this far.

You are to be congratulated for having survived the struggle it must have taken to get to this productive stage. Relatively few social enterprises succeed at this, and your experience and the insights you have picked up along the way need to be captured, documented, and distributed to others like you, folks who have the compassion, combined with the pragmatism, to go out and build something noble yet also sustainable.

It would be extremely useful for us to learn about your experiences, and even more useful to know which parts of this book you found worthwhile and which did not work for you. We plan to update the book over time based on reader feedback.

Please be in touch, and even more importantly, continue down the socially constructive path you have forged. You can write to us at whartondigitalpress@wharton.upenn.edu.

For updates, please visit wdp.wharton.upenn.edu/books/social-entrepreneurs-playbook.

Acknowledgments

This book would not have been possible but for the editorial and publication expertise and skills of Steve Kobrin, Shannon Berning, and Teresa Kocudak. Their insights, assistance, and patience turned this manuscript from a tedious tome into something social entrepreneurs out there are embracing and already aggressively using. The measure of their contribution lies not in the number of ebooks downloaded, but rather, in the number of humanitarians who have used the concepts in this book and thereby helped people in poverty and need. Without Steve, Shannon, and Teresa's ministrations, this change would not have happened.

Thanks to Whitney Peeling, whose publicity and PR skills were invaluable in helping us get the word out to the constituencies that mattered so much to us—all those folks working on reducing the distress of the so many people round the world.

Thanks to Roz Cohen and the team of students she managed, including Ravi Bellur, Samantha Fox, Sooreen Lee, Yuchen Luo, Danielle Matsumoto, Beth Mlynarczk, Roberto Sanabria, David Segal, Farah Shah, Serena Shi, May Sripatanaskul, Nancy Trinh, Ava Zhang, and Darya Zmachynskaya, all of whom helped us with the research, the analytics, the discovery-driven plans, and the fieldwork needed to help create and execute our field projects.

In particular, thanks to Christopher Wilfong for his outstanding contribution to the Zambia Feeds project in the development and implementation of the linear program and logistics planning tools. Also to Sarah Ryerson for her significant contribution to the performance of the clinic in the AidsAid project.

We would like to thank the following people who reviewed the work and our documents as they evolved and provided significant commentary and insight that helped shape the direction and voice of our manuscript: Allison Berliner, Benjamin Bruckman, Daniel

Cauley, Jeanne Chen, Melissa Kushner, Mary McKay, Jennifer Ralston, Hayley Rosengarten, and CJ Wise.

Thanks also to Diana Dickinson for her commitment and support "on the ground."

Lynn Selhat's assistance in editing early drafts of the manuscript was invaluable.

Our deepest thanks to the Wharton alumni who have sponsored this program. In particular, the Ambani, Collins, Durrett, Gruber, Holekamp, Hurst, Meyer, Poole, Rosenstein, Snider, and Trone families for their interest, commitment, and willingness to support work in a space fraught with uncertainty.

The Social Entrepreneur's Playbook Advisory Group

We would also like to thank the following advisors who helped shape this book by taking a survey about the free book, *The Social Entrepreneur's Playbook: Pressure Test Your Start-Up Idea—Step 1.*

Mustapha Abokede
Isaac Aggrey
Nafis (Peter) Ahmed
Leena Al Olaimy
Faten Alqaseer
Holger W. Altvater
Jill Anick
Pankaj Aswal
Lisa Atiq, social entrepreneur
Anisha Atluri
Ivan Atuyambe
Elvis Austins, founder,
    SpellAfrica Initiative
Dr. Paolo Aversa, Cass
    Business School,
    City University, London
Elena Avramov
Daniel Kwadwo Bampoh
Matias R. Barletta
Oscar Castañón Barragán
Emily Behr
Aman Bhullar
Daniella Bien-Aime,
    adult educator, Facilitator, and
    Trainer
Juan Carlos Díaz Bilbao
Harlan S. Blynn

Giada Bono
Cory Bowman, Netter
    Center for Community
    Partnerships, University
    of Pennsylvania
Vicki R. Brackens, founder,
    World of Cheddar, LLC
Theresa Bradley
Karla Breceda
Miguel Bremer-Wirtig
Katherine Brown-Hoekstra
C. J. Brown
Greg Byrne, principal,
    The Three Little Pigs Co.
Andrés Gutiérrez Campos
Marc Carr
Meaghan M. Casey
Richard J. Catherall
Charles D. Chand
Lloyd Chang
Paulo Chikoti-Bandua
Myrto Chliova
Roy Coheb
David Conegliano
Harris Contos, DMD, MBA
Renee Crichlow MD, FAAFP
Nurfarini Daing

Manvir Dandona
Chirag Dave
Nestor Lopez de Arroyabe
    Detrick DeBurr
Guadalupe de la Mata
Rahul Dewanjee, founder,
    Xeronow.com
Derek DiGiacomo
Thomas Dokubo
Lindsey Dunn, Skills to Shine
Aron Dutta, global head,
    Capital Markets Strategy,
    Cisco Systems; board
    member, Verificient.com
Philipp Alexander Ebel
Eugene Eccli
Desmond D. Emanuel
Robert T. Esposito, Esq.
Mr. Varuna Eswer
David A. Eustice
Orion Falvey, cofounder,
    InVision Foundation
Abayomi Fawehinmi
Horace L. Flournoy
John Fox
Samantha Fox
Dennis Foy
Michael Francis
Elena Gaffurini
Julio César Reynaga Galeas
Andrés Garcia de Tuñon
Jorge Valdés Garciatorres, PMP
Forough Ghahremani
Elena Gilson
Myra Goldstein Brown
Chad Gomes
Jerome S. Gotangco
Ken Granderson

Nico Groenenberg
Gro Martin Gunnarsen
Anthony N. Haddad
Y. Julie Han
Ayaz Haniffa
Thomas Hardy
Ira Harkavy
Lawrence Heimowitz, CPA
R. Paul Herman, Wharton '89,
    CEO of HIP Investor, Inc.
Jonathan Ho
Edmundo Hoffens
Mark Horoszowski, cofounder,
    MovingWorlds
Darnley W. Howard
Lucia Huang
Ariel Huskins, Founder,
    25:40life.com
Cynthia Jaggi
Dhruvi Kanabar
Deepa Kapoor
Mutembei Kariuki
Emanuel R. Kastl
Rasin A. Immad Katta
John Yohan Kim
Sasibai Kimis
Julie King, principal,
    Galileo Agency
Vera Klauer
Keith Kohler
Dr. Jussi V. Koivisto
Pragna Kolli
Monika Konieczny
    Korbinian
Jon Korin, Wharton '76
Vikrant Kothari
Marcin Krasnowolski
Dr. Stavros D. Ktenas

Aruna Kulatunga
Gloria Lam
Rachel Laurie
James Law, Singapore
Natt Leelawat
Isaac Lemor
Eddie Ler
Trisonia Lewis
Henry C. Lin
Ernestine Liu
Kana Lea One Love
Johannes Luger
Robyn Lui
Benjamin Lütgebüter
Megan McDonald, member
  of the Board of Directors,
  Attention Deficit Disorder
  Resources
Cecelia McFadden
Rauf N. Mammadov
Martina Mangelsdorf
Sudhir B. Mankodi
David T. Matta
D. Bruce Merrifield
Gopal Metro
Marta Milkowska
Mary C. Miller, JD,
  SPHR, ACC
Michael Miller
Professor Richard T. Minoff
Deepam Mishra
Vija Mitha
Michele Modina
Eshita Mohanty
Suzanne Lashmet Montazer
Mehmet Fahri Muftuoglu
Brian Mullen
Abd-ul Muqtadirr

Dennis Nakamura,
  Up!Grader Institute,
  Sao Paulo, Brazil
Matthew Nelson, COO,
  GreatSchools
Phil Neo KJ
Eduardo Barclay Nihill
José A. Nistal
Bosun Olawore
Nicholas Ondrejka
Randie Espera Ongoco
Olu Oyesanmi, MD, MPH
Michael Paolini
Jerry Parkes, CEO, Injaro
  Agricultural Capital
  Holdings Limited,
  Accra, Ghana
Erica Peressini
Larry D. Perkins, PhD, MBA
John F. Possumato
Silvia Prastani
Tahir Qazi
Michael Radke
Vinay Varma Raja, director,
  OrgPEOPLE
Professor Manisha
  Rajadhyaksha
Brandale D. Randolph,
  executive director, Project
  Poverty, Wharton '98
Grant Regan
José J. Riera
Abid Rizvi
Sergei Rodionov
Juan Carlos Roldan
Richard S. Roque
Alberto Ruíz
Megan Metz Rye

Miguel Paredes Sadler
Samuel Safran
Crescelito Martin S. D. Salvador
Randy Samsel
James Schmeling, managing
  director and cofounder,
  Institute for Veterans and
  Military Families, Syracuse
  University
David R. Schwartz
Miguel Scordamaglia
Noman Ahmed Shaheer
Kate Sherwood,
  Execution Strategy
Marika Shioiri-Clark
Anant Shukla
Arvind Singh, founder,
  Aavishkaar Micro Venture
  Capital Fund, and social
  entrepreneur, Wharton AMP
Snehanand (Ravi) Sinha,
  chairperson, Centre for Social
  Innovation, @BIMTECH
Samaira A. Sirajee
Moses Soh
Jonas Solbach
David Souder
Christina S. O. Sprock
Param Sreekanth
Dr. Ravi Srinivasan
Karim Srouji
Susan D. Steiner
Sean Steinmarc
Cathy Stephenson
Emily V. Stone
Sabarinathan Swaminathan
Ferdinand Swart, MSc

Unmesh Tambwekar
Timothy M. Taylor
Trang Quynh Than
Brett C. Thibodeau
Paritosh Tiwari
Leanne Tobias, Managing
  Principal, Malachite LLC
Mingles Tsoi
Emmanouel Tzouvelekas
Omar Valdez
Gwen Vaughan
Tatiana Vdovina
Shwetank Verma, Esq.
S. C. Vijayakumaar
Mason Vollmer, agricultural
  director, Camphill Soltane,
  Glenmoore, PA
Vishal M. Vyas
Karen Wagner
Faith Wallace
Kathryln Wang
Arnold I. Weiss, DDS, MScD
Landon Wiedenman, founder,
  Profile Health Systems
Anne Wilmerding
C. J. Wise, chief operating
  officer, goodsFORgood, Inc.
David Richard Wistocki
Steven Woda, uKnow.com
Carlos Alberto Wolff
Don Woolridge
John G. Yedinak
Geoff Yenson
Banruo (Rock) Zhou
James Zhou
Konstantina Zoehrer
Mihai Zota

Notes

1 Frank H. Knight, *Risk, Uncertainty and Profit*, Boston: Hart, Schaffner and Marx, 1921. Later references to "near-Knightian" circumstances refer to those where almost anything can happen. In such high-uncertainty contexts, the range of values of the environmental variables impinging on possible outcomes is wide and, importantly, there is no way of assigning a probability to their value other than assuming all values in the range are equiprobable. In such situations, the model builder just does not know: so the initial management mindset must be characterized by the desire to reduce uncertainty to risk.

2 For confidentiality, identifying details have been changed.

3 William Foster and Jeffrey Bradach, "Should Nonprofits Seek Profits?" *Harvard Business Review* (Feb. 2005).

4 Ibid., p. 2.

5 Coimbatore Krishnarao Prahalad, *The Fortune at the Bottom of the Pyramid*, Philadelphia: Wharton School Publishing, 2004.

6 "Net revenues" simply means you get more revenues than the costs you incur.

7 M. H. Boisot and I. C. MacMillan, "Crossing Epistemological Boundaries: Managerial and Entrepreneurial Approaches to Knowledge Management," *Long Range Planning* 37, no. 6 (2004): 505–24.

8 J. D. Thompson and I. C. MacMillan, "Business Models: Creating New Markets and Societal Wealth," *Long Range Planning* 43, no. 2–3 (2010): 291–307; and J. D. Thompson and I. C. MacMillan, "Making Social Ventures Work," *Harvard Business Review* 9 (2010): 66–73.

9 We thank Sue Yun Chi and Acumen for sharing their Acumen case study on Ecotact.

10 WHO/UNICEF Joint Monitoring Programme for Water Supply and Sanitation, "Progress on Sanitation and Drinking Water: 2013 Update," http://www.wssinfo.org/fileadmin/user_upload/resources/JMPreport2013.pdf.

11 B. Steven Kerr, "On the Folly of Rewarding A, while Hoping for B," *Academy of Management Executive* (Feb. 1995): 9, 1; ABI/INFORM Global, p. 7.

12 *Free* is a loaded word in this case, because defecating in public places is actually not "free." It costs a society a great deal in terms of mortality and morbidity due to illness, lost productivity, and so on. Unfortunately, many people who defecate in public do so, first, because they have no other choice—their governments do not provide the basic waste infrastructures we take for granted in the West—and second, because they do not readily see the connection between their actions and the spread of disease.

13 This is one of the main reasons the Wharton Social Entrepreneurship Program prefers to work with intrapreneurial ventures.

14 See http://www.singerco.com/company/history%20?iframe=true&width= 100%&height=100%.

15 "CEMEX: Innovation in Housing for the Poor," Michigan Business School Case Study, Dec. 12, 2003.

16 Ibid.

17 John Paul, "Patrimonio Hoy: A Groundbreaking Corporate Program to Alleviate Mexico's Housing Crisis," NextBillion.net—Development Through Enterprise," NextBillion.net | Development through Enterprise, May 26, 2009.

18 Rita Gunther McGrath and Ian C MacMillan, *MarketBusters*, Cambridge, MA: Harvard Business School Press, 2005.

19 Our thanks to Jeanne Chen for this quote.

20 For confidentiality, the social entrepreneur's name and other identifying details have been changed.

21 Alexander Osterwalder, Yves Pigneur, Alan Smith (and 470 practitioners from 45 countries), *Business Model Generation*, Hoboken, NJ: John Wiley and Sons, 2010.

22 R. G. McGrath and I. C. MacMillan, "Discovery-Driven Planning," *Harvard Business Review* 73, no. 4 (1995): 44–54.

23 Return on sales (ROS): A ratio widely used to evaluate a company's operational efficiency, ROS is also known as a firm's "operating profit margin." Calculated by dividing the profits of the business by the total revenues generated.

24 Return on assets (ROA): A performance measure used to evaluate the efficiency of the firm's assets, ROA is calculated by dividing the profits from the business by the total assets (e.g., equipment, buildings, inventory).

25 You should do your DDP based on what you expect to be happening three to five years after start-up, *not* performance at start-up. *Only* if the three- to five-year targets seem doable, then and only then, should you go to the effort of the detailed planning of the launch. If they do not look doable in three to five years, drop the project.

26 Rita Gunther McGrath and Ian C. MacMillan, *Discovery-Driven Growth: A Breakthrough Process to Reduce Risk and Seize Opportunity*, Cambridge, MA: Harvard Business School Press, 2009.

27 Ibid.

28 Clayton Christensen, Scott Cook, and Taddy Hall, "Marketing Malpractice: The Cause and the Cure," *Harvard Business Review* 83, no. 12 (Dec. 2005).

29 B. M. Staw, "Knee-Deep in the Big Muddy: A Study of Escalating Commitment to a Chosen Course of Action," *Organizational Behavior and Human Performance* 16 (1978): 27–44.

Index

About the Authors

Ian (Mac) C. MacMillan is the academic director of the Sol C. Snider Entrepreneurial Research Center and Dhirubhai Ambani Professor of Entrepreneurship and Innovation at the Wharton School, University of Pennsylvania.

Mac has taught at Columbia University, New York University, Northwestern University, and the University of South Africa. Prior to joining the academic world, he was a chemical engineer, and gained experience in gold and uranium mines, chemical and explosives factories, oil refineries, soap and food manufacturers, and the South African Atomic Energy Board. He has also been a director of companies in the travel, import-export, and pharmaceutical fields in the United States, South Africa, Canada, Hong Kong, and Japan. Mac is the author or a coauthor of books and articles on new ventures, innovation, organizational politics, and strategy formulation. His articles have appeared in *Harvard Business Review* and *Sloan Management Review*. He is coauthor of the bestselling books *Corporate Venturing, The Entrepreneurial Mindset, Market Busters, Unlocking Opportunities for Growth*, and *Discovery-Driven Growth*.

James D. Thompson is cofounder and director of the Wharton Social Entrepreneurship Program. His areas of research focus are social entrepreneurship, building future markets, and investment under conditions of high, or near-Knightian, uncertainty.

Jim teaches in Wharton Executive Education programs and works with management teams around the world to design and execute organic growth strategies that increase the value of their firms. Prior to joining the academic world, he was a divisional director of a public company, responsible for business unit turnarounds and new market development. He currently serves on the executive board of a venture capital–funded company in Philadelphia and served on the investment advisory committee of a Swiss social entrepreneurship investment fund.

Jim holds a PhD from EPFL (École Polytechnique Fédérale de Lausanne) and has been published in the *Harvard Business Review*, *Journal of Management*, *Long Range Planning*, *Management Science*, *Organization Science*, and the *Research-Technology Management Journal*. He is a recipient of Best Paper Awards in innovation by the European Business School and the Thought Leader category of the Entrepreneurship Division at the U.S. Academy of Management.

About Wharton Digital Press

Wharton Digital Press was established to inspire bold, insightful thinking within the global business community. In the tradition of The Wharton School of the University of Pennsylvania and its online business journal, *Knowledge@Wharton*, Wharton Digital Press uses innovative digital technologies to help managers meet the challenges of today and tomorrow.

As an entrepreneurial publisher, Wharton Digital Press delivers relevant, accessible, conceptually sound, and empirically based business knowledge to readers wherever and whenever they need it. Its format ranges from ebooks to print books available through print-on-demand technology. Directed to a general business audience, the Press's areas of interest include management and strategy, innovation and entrepreneurship, finance and investment, leadership, marketing, operations, human resources, social responsibility, and business-government relations.

wdp.wharton.upenn.edu

About The Wharton School

Founded in 1881 as the first collegiate business school, The Wharton School of the University of Pennsylvania is recognized globally for intellectual leadership and ongoing innovation across every major discipline of business education. With a broad global community and one of the most published business school faculties, Wharton creates ongoing economic and social value around the world. The School has 5,000 undergraduate, MBA, executive MBA, and doctoral students; more than 9,000 annual participants in executive education programs; and a powerful alumni network of 92,000 graduates.

www.wharton.upenn.edu